# HUMAN RESOURCE DEVELOPMENT

## The New Trainer's Guide

### Second Edition

## Les Donaldson

## Edward E. Scannell

**ADDISON-WESLEY PUBLISHING COMPANY, INC.**

Reading, Massachusetts • Menlo Park, California
Don Mills, Ontario • Wokingham, England • Amsterdam • Bonn
Sydney • Singapore • Tokyo • Madrid • Bogotá
Santiago • San Juan

Figure I–1, Human Resource Wheel, is adapted by permission from *Models of Excellence,* 1983, The American Society for Training and Development. Permission is also granted for material on pages 6–7, (the definition of training and development and the Fifteen Key Training and Development Roles).

Figure 6–1, Rated Effectiveness of Training Methods, is from Stephen J. Carroll, Jr., Frank T. Paine, and John J. Ivancevich, "The Relative Effectiveness of Training Methods—Expert Opinion and Research," *Personnel Psychology,* 25:495–509, 1972, and is reprinted with permission.

Figure 6–2, Perceived Effectiveness of Nine Training Methods for Six Objectives, is from John W. Newstrom, "Evaluating the Effectiveness of Training Methods." It appeared in the January 1980 issue of *The Personnel Administrator* and is reprinted with permission.

Figure 14–1, Meeting Planners Function Sheet, is adapted with permission from Meeting Planners International.

The Session Evaluation on page 170 is reprinted with permission from The American Society for Training and Development.

The ASTD Reaction Sheet on page 171 is reprinted with permission from The American Society for Training and Development.

The MPI Course Evaluation Form on page 172 is reprinted with permission from Meeting Planners International.

The 1984 ASTD Conference Evaluation form on page 173 is reprinted with permission from The American Society for Training and Development.

**Library of Congress Cataloging-in-Publication Data**

Donaldson, Les, 1928–
  Human resource development.

  1. Group relations training.  I. Scannell, Edward E.
II. Title.
HM133.D64   1986    158′.2    86-7934
ISBN 0-201-03087-X

Cover design by Steve Snider
Text design by Kenneth J. Wilson
Set in 10-point Times Roman by Modern Graphics, Inc., Weymouth, MA

BCDEFGHIJ-AL-987

*Second Printing, March 1987*

# CONTENTS

## Contents

# Contents

# Contents

# Contents

# ACKNOWLEDGMENTS

A project like this is always a joint effort. While the authors take full responsibility for its coverage or its omissions, there are a number of people who knowingly and unknowingly contributed to its content.

To the hundreds of participants who took part in seminars conducted by the authors and helped field test the material, we are very grateful. To our fellow ASTD members across the country who gave us ideas and encouraged us to write this type of book, we are equally indebted.

Special thanks go to Betty Norris, Kim Dean, and Tessie Ballard who waded through hundreds of pages of scribbled and rewritten drafts and managed to come out with this handsomely refined manuscript.

# PREFACE

*How was the session?*
*Well, first of all, he read his materials to us.*
*That's bad.*
*Yeah—and secondly, he read it poorly.*
*That's worse.*
*Right—but thirdly, it wasn't worth reading.*

This scenario would be humorous if it were not so realistic. Unfortunately, though, it seems that every trainer, every meeting planner, every chairperson—indeed, every*body*—has witnessed such an incident at one time or another.

Like its first edition, this revised book is written primarily for our newer training colleagues. Like its predecessor, it is intended to be a practical "how to" manual. While this book is addressed to the new trainer, the more experienced trainer will also find its contents useful as a review and refresher. Although not specifically addressed to the academic market, it has been used extensively in college and university classes as a reference source for both undergraduate and graduate courses in human resource development.

Both authors have conducted numerous "train-the-trainer" programs across the country. Because these sessions have been learning experiences for us, we have tried to transform those experiences onto these pages. It is our intent that the lessons we have learned with—and from—our colleagues might be reflected and related in these chapters.

The material in this publication has been field-tested in hundreds of training programs, and the many suggestions and ideas of trainees and trainers have been incorporated in this revision. Regardless of your experiences (or lack thereof!) in human resource development, you'll find dozens of real-world examples that will work for you. Whether your training responsibilities are in the areas of technical training, skills, sales, management, organizational development, or dozens of other relevant disciplines, this book offers you workable and pragmatic tips and techniques to add to your "trainer's tool kit."

If you are a new trainer, you'll find this book a self-development guide.

The contents are arranged in a step-by-step process so that you can indeed "learn by doing."

The chapters are arranged to correspond to the actual approach and sequences a trainer would develop in designing a training program. Use the tips offered to assist you in designing, developing, and delivering your own program.

The more experienced facilitator will find this book a handy reference guide that attempts to offer the best of two worlds. Theory-based educational and learning principles, coupled with sound educational psychology, are blended with the practicality of cost-effective training techniques. New (or even forgotten!) concepts or philosophy may trigger additional thoughts and ideas about a variety of training applications.

Our objective is to give the novice and the experienced trainer a down-to-earth "cookbook" of workable ideas for the preparation and presentation of productive training sessions.

LES DONALDSON
EDWARD E. SCANNELL

# INTRODUCTION

*What does your daddy do?*
*I think he develops human race horses.*

Human resource development (HRD) has been growing at an astonishing rate both in the United States and around the world. A recent report by the Bureau of Labor Statistics identifies HRD as the fastest growing profession in America.

In the last few years, the field of human resource development has been growing at an astronomical rate in the United States. Today's estimates place training expenditures in the United States at well over $100 billion annually. While this may sound like an exceedingly high amount to many of us, some authorities contend that this figure still undervalues the total costs! A 1986 ASTD publication, *Serving The New Corporation*, states that the figure spent on training and development approximates $210 billion annually. Some authorities estimate that over one million people in America spend a portion of their time performing training and development activities. Of this number, it is further estimated that around 200,000 of us are full-time trainers.

The American Society for Training and Development, the world's largest professional organization devoted to the development of human resources, has continually addressed itself to a further definition of the field. In its *Models for Excellence*, a 1983 publication identifying competencies for the profession, nine human resource practice areas were identified. These are shown in the Human Resource Wheel (Figure I-1).

Human resource development is an exciting career field that provides many opportunities for trainers to grow and develop their skills. Because of the variety of activities involved in training, there is no reason for a trainer to become bored. Researching, analyzing, writing, training, leading group meetings, and platform speaking are among the various assignments that both new and experienced trainers perform.

The recent productivity crisis caused many chief executive officers to realize and acknowledge that the productivity problem was also a "people problem." Today, more than ever before, managers realize that the long-term success of any organization is tied closely to employee training and development. To be prepared for rapidly changing conditions and normal

1

**Figure I-1.** Human Resource Wheel

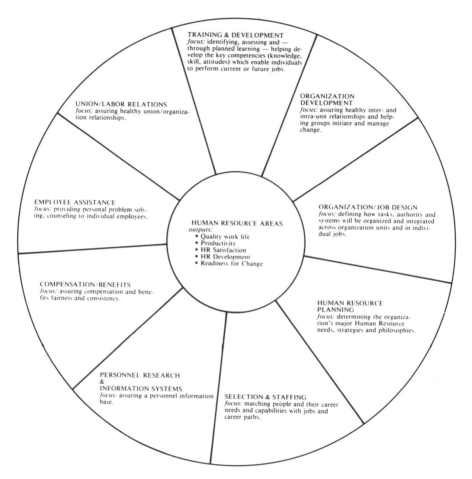

TRAINING & DEVELOPMENT
*focus:* identifying, assessing and — through planned learning — helping develop the key competencies (knowledge, skill, attitudes) which enable individuals to perform current or future jobs.

ORGANIZATION DEVELOPMENT
*focus:* assuring healthy inter- and intra-unit relationships and helping groups initiate and manage change.

UNION/LABOR RELATIONS
*focus:* assuring healthy union/organization relationships.

EMPLOYEE ASSISTANCE
*focus:* providing personal problem solving, counseling to individual employees.

HUMAN RESOURCE AREAS
*outputs:*
• Quality work life
• Productivity
• HR Satisfaction
• HR Development
• Readiness for Change

ORGANIZATION/JOB DESIGN
*focus:* defining how tasks, authority and systems will be organized and integrated across organization units and in individual jobs.

COMPENSATION/BENEFITS
*focus:* assuring compensation and benefits fairness and consistency.

HUMAN RESOURCE PLANNING
*focus:* determining the organization's major Human Resource needs, strategies and philosophies.

PERSONNEL RESEARCH & INFORMATION SYSTEMS
*focus:* assuring a personnel information base.

SELECTION & STAFFING
*focus:* matching people and their career needs and capabilities with jobs and career paths.

attrition, each organization must provide training for its employees. Thus, training is a continuing process that spans the employee's career.

As management comes to see the value of human resource development, the training generalist and specialist become more valuable. The individual entering this dynamic field can look forward to a personally rewarding career. New trainers are given an opportunity to develop skills in dealing with people. They learn to communicate, influence, and develop cooperative relationships in an open and candid way. These human skills enhance the new trainer's effectiveness in all dealings with people.

The trainer's opportunities to learn and grow are unlimited. The social and behavioral sciences offer ample research findings for the most ambitious trainers to study, synthesize, and integrate into their training programs. A diligent study of traditional training techniques combined with the willingness to keep an open mind to absorb new findings will help the new trainer become a professional.

This book is intended as a "how to" book for the new practitioner. The lack of footnotes in no way indicates a bypassing of academic research, but shows only that we believe our reader is more interested in practicality than theory. This is the basic premise of our work.

In Chapter 1, you'll gain insight into the field of Human Resource Development (HRD) and the various functions that trainers perform. You will get an overview of the many roles and responsibilities of a trainer and the goals that the human resource developer attempts to achieve.

Chapter 2 covers the design of a training program. We provide a step-by-step method of all the elements that are essential in construction of a viable learning experience—from the diagnosis of problems through needs analysis and the development of training objectives, all the way through to the selection of evaluation criteria. By following these steps, you can be sure that your program will be an effective one.

In Chapter 3, you will learn how to determine what training is really needed and how to write a training proposal.

Chapter 4 covers instructional and behavioral objectives, relating the need for long-term training programs to the objectives of the program. This chapter also includes a sample task analysis.

Lesson planning is our subject for Chapter 5. Here you will learn how to write a usable outline and you can adopt one of the sample forms to your own use.

In Chapter 6, we concentrate on methods of instruction. You will learn advantages and disadvantages of several commonly used techniques.

In Chapter 7, you will see how the proper use of a wide variety of visual aids can increase your presentation skills and help your trainees understand the topic of discussion. A few "tricks of the trade" will show you some excellent ways to become skilled with visuals.

Computer-Based Instruction (CBI) has already made its mark in HRD and is our subject for Chapter 8.

Chapter 9 covers the role of communication in training. You will readily see that the best-prepared material in the world is literally worthless if it cannot be efficiently and effectively communicated to your audiences.

Chapter 10 covers adult learning theory and some basic laws of learning. We discuss and explain adult learning principles that have been found to be most effective in training. You'll see that the proper application of sound theory makes for good practice!

Chapter 11 is devoted to motivation theory reviewed from a theoretical and practical basis and then related to new techniques that improve learning and increase productivity.

Facilitation skills form the subject matter of Chapter 12. You will see that a changing role for training professionals is that of a facilitator of learning. Effective questioning techniques are also included.

Chapter 13, covering presentation skills, offers a number of proven platform techniques that will materially enhance your public-speaking activities.

Chapter 14 describes the steps in planning a meeting. You'll understand why some meetings fail and how to make sure that yours don't.

In Chapter 15, you will learn how to conduct successful meetings. You'll see how to "break the ice," build interest, and, in general, become a proficient meeting planner.

Problem participants are the subject for Chapter 16. We describe different types of behaviors sometimes presented by trainees and offer suggestions on the tactful handling of these potentially disruptive behaviors.

Chapter 17 outlines step-by-step directions for program evaluation. Several formats are included that can be modified for your own use.

Chapter 18 provides an overview of the professional trainer. The qualities of both the "All Star" and the "Falling Star" trainers are covered. As a review, several tested ideas regarding better training are proposed.

The chapters of this book are built in a sequence similar to an actual training program. The many new concepts presented in the following pages can help you as you enter the dynamic field of human resource development!

# CHAPTER 1

# So You're Going to Be a Trainer

*Welcome to our world!*

Human resource development is an exciting and important challenge. Working with people and helping them grow and develop—both personally and professionally—will bring mutually rewarding results. At Disney University (the training center for Disneyworld), one sees this statement of Walt Disney, "Anyone can dream, design, and create the most wonderful place in the world, but it takes people to make that dream a reality." That's really what human resource development is all about—working with people.

Your decision to become a trainer means you will become a change agent. You will facilitate a transfer of knowledge or skills to people who will use what they learn to change their behavior. You may start by giving orientation sessions to new employees. Next you may become involved in preparing and conducting basic training programs for people starting new assignments or people whose job requirements have changed due to the introduction of new systems or new machines. After you have developed your training skills through experience with entry-level assignments, you may be given an opportunity to research, design, test, and conduct advanced training programs intended to increase productivity and employee development.

The changes you facilitate should always lead to growth for the trainees, growth that will make them more effective people. You will feel a sense of personal accomplishment when you see these changes transformed into increases in productivity. You will share in the satisfaction and pride developed by employees as their confidence grows.

Training senior or professional employees presents special challenges. The senior employee participating in a training workshop is looking for something new. Because many senior employees may need to review the basic techniques associated with their work, the trainer must find a way to

5

present introductory training in such a way that it does not appear simplistic. Often you can accomplish this by using participative techniques to explain a new application or innovation.

This chapter will provide an overview of training and development. You'll learn how to approach management for support and how to secure management's interest in your program. You'll also be given guidelines for your own self-development so that you can progress more rapidly in your career. Throughout the chapter, you'll be given introductory guidelines for developing yourself and other people.

## WHAT DO TRAINERS DO?

As indicated earlier, the American Society for Training and Development Competency study, *Models for Excellence,* offers an in-depth profile of the varied roles and responsibilities of training and development positions. The study provides a thorough discussion of the field and presents a standard of professional performance.

Simply stated, the study defines the main focus of training and development as "identifying, assessing—and through planned learning—helping develop the key competences which enable individuals to perform current or future jobs."

It is interesting to note the continuing contributions of Leonard Nadler of George Washington University. One of the most respected individuals in our field, Dr. Nadler has been using the now-popular term human resource development since 1969. He defines HRD as "organized learning experiences in a definite time period to increase the possibility of improving job performance growth."

The ASTD study suggests that people engaged in training and development perform different types of activities. The fifteen key roles listed here are the major functions involved in training and development. It is important to note that these are roles and do not describe jobs, that is, a particular job will often be comprised of multiple roles.

*Evaluator.* The role of identifying the extent of the impact of a program, service, or product.

*Group Facilitator.* The role of managing group discussion and group process so that individuals learn and group members feel the experience is positive.

*Individual Development Counselor.* The role of helping an individual assess personal competencies, values, and goals, as well as plan development and career actions.

*Instructional Writer.* The role of preparing written learning and instructional materials.

6

*Instructor.* The role of presenting information and directing structured learning experiences so that individuals learn.

*Manager of Training and Development.* The role of planning, organizing, staffing, controlling training and development operations or training and development projects, and linking training and development operations with other organization units.

*Marketer.* The role of selling training and development viewpoints, learning packages, programs, and services to target audiences outside one's own work unit.

*Media Specialist.* The role of producing software for and using audio, visual, computer, and other hardware-based technologies for training and development.

*Needs Analyst.* The role of defining gaps between ideal and actual performance and specifying the cause of the gaps.

*Program Administrator.* The role of ensuring that the facilities, equipment, materials, participants, and other components of a learning event are present and that program logistics run smoothly.

*Program Designer.* The role of preparing objectives, defining content, and selecting and sequencing activities for a specific program.

*Strategist.* The role of developing long-range plans for what the training and development structure, organization, direction, policies, programs, services, and practices will be in order to accomplish the training and development mission.

*Task Analyst.* Identifying activities, tasks, subtasks, and human resource and support requirements necessary to attain specific results in a job or organization.

*Theoretician.* The role of developing and testing theories of learning, training, and development.

*Transfer Agent.* The role of helping individuals apply new learning to their work tasks.

## THE STAGES OF TRAINING AND DEVELOPMENT

A sequential approach to our planned learning experiences is outlined in this section.

As shown here, the matrix begins with Stage 1, called the Unconscious Incompetent.

| Stage 1<br><br>*Unconscious*<br>*Incompetent* | Stage 3<br><br>*Conscious*<br>*Competent* |
|---|---|
| Stage 2<br><br>*Conscious*<br>*Incompetent* | Stage 4<br><br>*Unconscious*<br>*Competent* |

The Unconscious Incompetent is a person who lacks the required skills, knowledge, or attitudes but is not even aware of this void. This is a person who "doesn't know he/she doesn't know." Or, more crudely, "They're dumb, but they don't know it."

Stage 2, called the Conscious Incompetent, is the next progression. It means the individual still lacks the necessary skills or knowledge, but at least he/she is aware of this situation. To put it bluntly, "They're still dumb, but they know it."

Perhaps as the result of a training or developmental experience, an individual may move to Stage 3, the Conscious Competent. This refers to the person who has acquired some "smarts" and in fact has achieved a satisfactory level of competence or even expertise in a given area. This is the person "who's smart and knows it."

Finally, Stage 4 is called the Unconscious Competent. As a person becomes even more skilled or gains even more knowledge, he/she may become so expert in a particular area that it becomes almost a habit. In other words, behavior and action are almost automatic, requiring little conscious thought or effort. A person may do a thing unconsciously, but do it very well.

As an example, think back to your early teens. When you were taken for a car ride, the driver performed all the necessary operations and you were merely "along for the ride." As you approached driving age, you probably focused your attention on learning the details of motor vehicle operation. Doubtless, you were very much aware of what you didn't know (Conscious Incompetent). Through a patient parent, sibling, friend, or teacher, you slowly began to learn, through study and practice, the safe and proper details of driving. Soon, you became (and hopefully still are) a good, if not excellent, driver. You were consciously aware (Stage 3) of your competence.

If you drove your car to the office today, try to recall the exact and precise sequence of what happened from the time you got into the car until you walked into your office. If you're like most of us, you know you got there, but you're not really quite certain how! You would really have to think hard to remember all the steps. You probably drove to the office without even thinking about it. Your skills are such that you performed a myriad of tasks in a most competent manner (Stage 4).

The need for training is most obvious in Stage 2. While there may be no problem in Stage 3, it would appear that the problem in Stage 1 is one of selection and Stage 4 that of motivation.

## DEVELOPING OTHERS

We often forget that trainees or seminar participants may need help to develop themselves. As trainers we can facilitate that process by determining what skills and areas of knowledge are lacking in the organization and then designing and conducting training programs to correct those deficiencies. The individual participants, however, must have the desire to improve and be willing to apply themselves to the training program. You, as a trainer, can influence the participants' decisions by establishing an empathetic relationship in the classroom.

New and senior employees alike need empathy and understanding in a new situation. A senior employee who has not attended a training session for a number of years may be at a disadvantage trying to compete with a recently graduated employee. Fear may even be a factor. New material may be easier for the academically oriented new employee to handle than for the work-oriented senior employee. You can reduce these problems for senior employees by eliminating unnecessary competition and by showing empathy for them as well as for the other participants.

You can show that you empathize with a participant by relating a similar incident that you have experienced. Try to remember such situations and how you reacted. Try to recapture that feeling and express it to the group. Comment on your understanding of the concerns and problems of the participants and offer to help with any problems that come up during the program. Climate-setting activities or ice-breakers are excellent ways to establish a comfort zone.

## PLANNING YOUR SELF-DEVELOPMENT

Any experienced trainer will tell you that all development is self-development. People must ultimately take responsibility for their own training if they are to become professionals. It is important to realize that personal development is a very individual process. Research has shown that all individuals learn in specific ways and at different rates. One person may learn better by reading, one by attending a lecture, and another by some form of involvement.

Only one person can determine the best system for you, and that person is you. Find the system or combination of learning systems that you enjoy most, for it will probably be the most effective for your particular growth and development.

Once you accept the fact that the final responsibility for your development rests with you, you are on your way to success. All you have to do is organize a plan and work toward achieving the objectives of that plan.

### Organizing a Plan

Your plan should include a balanced accumulation of knowledge and skills. By following a structured method for developing specific goals, you can organize a plan that will fit your personal goals. You may need to do some homework to determine skills you wish to master at the various stages of your program.

The following list of basic skills for trainers may help you to establish your plan:

- Analyzing performance problems to determine any applicable training and development solutions

- Identifying training needs

- Identifying skills and knowledge requirements of jobs

- Assessing performance before and after training

- Establishing behavioral objectives for programs

- Designing training programs

- Determining program content

- Applying adult learning theory in developing programs

- Evaluating instructional methods

- Developing training materials

- Determining program structure

- Revising programs based on evaluation feedback

- Conducting training programs

- Conducting on-the-job training

- Using simulation and gaming techniques

- Arranging program logistics (facilities, lodging, meals, etc.)

- Preparing budgets

- Evaluating proposals from outside consultants

- Establishing good working relationships with managers

- Making formal management presentation

- Learning about the organization

- Establishing rapport with key personnel

- Conducting strategic planning

- Attending seminars and conferences for personal development

- Communicating effectively

Review these items. On a separate sheet of paper, list the top ten skills you wish to master.

Ideas and information about most of these subjects will be covered in succeeding chapters.

### Following a Systematic Learning Approach

Two research findings provide the basis for an on-the-job program of personal development. The first is that people learn more readily when they can use the information as they perform their jobs. The second is that the most significant part of people's development results from their association with one particular superior on the job.

The implications are clear. Plan your development around your current job and study the techniques used by your superior. When you use these two guidelines as the framework for your development, you can devise a learning system that will have a very high probability of success.

The following steps will help you establish a systematic approach to self-development:

1. Analyze yourself, your current job, and the job you want in the future.

2. Consider your current level of expertise and write a goal that will help you achieve the future job.

3. Write a developmental career path that includes your current job requirements and identify those components of the future job that are similar to components of your current job.

4. Arrange the job components in order of priority in relation to the immediate job requirements and the long-term accomplishments of your goals.

5. Establish a sequence for learning the job components in their order of priority.

6. Make a list of possible obstacles to the achievement of your objectives.

7. Make a list of people and other resources that you will need to support your efforts.

8. Write your final objective with dates of accomplishment for each component part.

9. Test the objective against these criteria: Is it reasonable, achievable, measurable, timely, and can it be evaluated?

## SELLING TRAINING TO MANAGEMENT

Training departments exist as management tools to be used in the accomplishment of management goals. If we remember that our function is to serve management, our results will be greater because management will support programs directed at its goals. The most productive step a trainer can take is the step that leads to management support.

### Determining the Priorities of Management

The first step in gaining the support of management is to determine management's priorities. You must determine what training is needed to provide the skills or knowledge necessary to reach the objectives established by those priorities. You first have to determine what is needed and then what will be authorized.

Usually a questionnaire or phone survey is used to obtain opinions from field and lower-level managers. Once a list of needs has been developed from the field management survey, it is compared with top-management priorities. Those needs that fit management priorities are used to determine training needs.

### Soliciting Support and Commitment

To ensure management support, involve managers in a discussion of how the training will affect their objectives. Then, outline programs to fulfill the training needs and present them to management for approval. Include cost estimates as well as estimates of results of the training. Although overused, the term "bottom line" still captures the attention of management.

A candid discussion of budgets, including overhead and additional expenses, if related to the expected results, will preclude later rejection of the program. Everything that is covered up front will ensure management's support throughout the program. Explain what can reasonably be expected and the type of management support needed in order to get the expected results.

Many training programs have failed because managers were trained to act in a people-oriented way but were then rewarded for acting differently. For example, in one company first level supervisors were instructed to include employees in the planning process. However, the managers who evaluated these supervisors ignored this plan and used other criteria for appraisal. Management must be asked to support the new behavioral changes with policies and actions that reward the new behavior.

### Planning Specific Follow-up Procedures

The support of top management is absolutely necessary to implement follow-up procedures. First, determination of reduced costs, improved productivity, and increased profits requires access to records and reports. Further, management policies and procedures must be implemented to institutionalize the changes brought about by training. Personal objectives of the trainees should involve the use of new skills. Salary increases and promotions should also be based on the use of new skills.

In the case of management development programs, top management should set the example. If they use the new skills, lower-level management will emulate their actions. If lower-level management sees the participation and involvement of top management, they will recognize that the new system or new skills are important. Top management's support of a training objective is best expressed when they promote individuals who used the new skills to improve their results.

### SUMMARY

You are ready to embark on a truly exciting journey into the field of human resource development. It is an area where people serve people. With a variety of roles and responsibilities, you are certain to find an area of practice compatible to your own interests and expertise. So set your sights and analyze your own plan for self-development. We feel certain the following chapters can help you become a skilled and productive trainer.

# CHAPTER 2

# Designing Effective Training Programs

*Let's start at the very beginning.*

In looking at the many ingredients that make a training program an effective one, the task of blending these elements can be likened to that of a skilled chef. The finished product of the culinary professional—like the end result of the HRD professional—depends on the correct mix and the artful use of the proper ingredients.

To be effective, a training program must be result oriented. A knowledge of the many activities and processes involved will help you design a productive and viable learning experience. You can assure an effective program by developing objectives and evaluation criteria for the results expected. Moreover, each element of the program design must be weighed against the expected results. Too many training programs seem to be designed and conducted with little, if any, attention paid to results or evaluation. Evaluation is an ongoing process that begins even before the first thoughts of training.

The idea is not that we consider evaluation as the first step, but rather that it overrides and provides the framework for all the activities in the total human resource development program. As we consider a particular training request, we might first evaluate the request by asking if training is what is really needed. Experienced training directors often find that well-intentioned but misinformed colleagues may assume that all problems are training problems and, therefore, can be solved by a training program.

In this chapter, we describe a step-by-step approach that will help ensure your success in designing training programs. We will cover problem diagnosis to determine the necessity for training. Next, you will see how to define training goals in terms of specific objectives that can be evaluated. Various instructional techniques will be covered, and you will learn to match them with specific training problems. We'll discuss techniques that gain participant involvement and result in a favorable learning climate. Finally, we will cover methods for determining evaluation criteria.

## A SYSTEMS APPROACH

Training is much more complicated than simply telling or showing someone how to perform a task. Training is an attempt to transfer skills and knowledge to trainees in such a way that the trainees accept and use those skills in the performance of their jobs. The knowledge or skill should be specific, and the training should be directed at identified behavioral change. The trainer should learn specific skills or techniques that can be demonstrated and observed on the job. There are several steps that can be used in designing training programs that will accomplish these goals.

### Conduct Needs Analysis

The first step, conducting a needs analysis, is the most important. Experts in problem solving agree that a problem well defined is half solved! Too often, our training colleagues pull out an "off-the-shelf" program without really knowing what the real cause of a training problem may be.

Training is not the answer to every organizational problem. Even the most proficient and experienced group of employees will have problems in their operations. When a problem arises, it must be thoroughly diagnosed before training is prescribed as the best solution. Many problems are caused by conditions that are not affected by people. The most proficient work force cannot keep producing when there are no raw materials available.

Determining training needs can be time-consuming, but the investment will pay off in a better planned program. Even when the problem is caused by people, you must analyze the situation to determine what kind of a problem you are dealing with. For example, the problem may relate to lack of knowledge. The person simply may not know what to do. These types of problems are called cognitive problems.

You may find that the problem is one of a skill deficiency. An operator may know what to do but may not know how to do it. More likely, however, that operator may not know how to do it at a highly proficient level. Your training design will then be directed to bringing people up to acceptable levels of proficiency. These problems are called psychomotor problems.

Often you will find a deficiency in spite of the fact that conditions of the situation seem highly conducive to high productivity. The problem may be related to the individual's attitudes. He or she may be skilled but, for a variety of reasons, "just doesn't care." These problems are in the affective domain.

15

Checking each of these three areas will help you find the real problem and determine the proper training to alleviate it. By carefully analyzing the situation, you can determine what role, if any, training should play in solving the problem.

You must carefully collect and analyze all the data you can find relevant to the actual work situation. Through research and observation, you will gather job descriptions, task analyses, and other information pertinent to the situation for which training is being proposed. These will include individual and organizational needs, both current and future—in short, anything and everything that is directly or remotely connected to the task at hand.

At this point, you will begin to identify those areas where training will assist. Some areas, of course, will obviously be appropriate for the training function. Others may be far afield from the realm of training.

## Determine Training Requirements

In order to determine whether or not training plays a role in a problem solution, you must closely examine the problem. We have found the following approach very effective for this purpose.

1. Develop an overview of the problem.

2. Examine all changes that have occurred just prior to the emergence of the problem.

3. List the most likely causes of the problem.

4. Evaluate the role training can play in solving the problem.

## Determine Objectives and Standards

"The best laid plans of mice and men. . . ." This oft-used quote aptly describes the dilemma in which trainers often find themselves. Elaborately designed and executed training programs may fail if they are not goal directed. The program may even receive praise from the participants as being innovative and informative, and still fail to result in behavioral change. You can avoid this problem by incorporating specific goals and objectives into the training design.

A training objective is distinguished from a training goal in that the objective defines a level of performance in terms of quantity (for example, the number of units of output per time frame) and the specific quality of the performance, whereas a training goal is defined as a general skill or behavioral change that occurs as the final result of the training.

Unless we know what it is that we want our development program to do, how can we possibly measure its success? Using behavioral terms, we spell out the desired behavior and performance standards the program purports to achieve.

### Develop Course Content

Now you are ready to build the curriculum that should be covered in the program. Recognizing the restraints that may be imposed (time, resources, budgets, etc.), your task is to separate the "need to know" from the "nice to know."

After selecting and sequencing your material, identify the minimum basic subject matter required to satisfy the stated objectives. Then compare and contrast the parameters of training time available—or required—and adjust accordingly.

### Select Instructional Methods and Media

Once specific objectives have been developed, you can select the training methods most likely to be effective in achieving those objectives. There are a number of training methods to choose from. Lectures, role plays, case studies, games, and group discussions are all useful in specific situations. Each method must be evaluated in relation to your objective.

Each instructional method has its pros and cons. Your task is to identify the methods best suited to meet your objectives. Skillful blending of methods and visual media will help ensure your attainment of identified goals.

You must know something about your trainees to determine which techniques will be most effective. Have the trainees been exposed to classroom training before or has all their training been conducted on the job? Are they familiar enough with the concept to discuss the problem and develop group answers or will they need input from you? Are there natural leaders in the group or must you provide step-by-step instructions? Do they have the basic knowledge to approach the problem or must you provide guidelines to keep them on the track?

The participants' willingness, desire, and readiness to learn will affect your training techniques. If participants are highly motivated when they arrive in the training room, you have no problem. If they don't want to be there or if they feel they can't learn anything, then you must use training techniques that build interest and desire to learn. You must develop a climate in which they will become motivated to participate and learn.

### Perform Test Run

After you have completed your program design, gather your associates together for a test run. Conduct the program for them just as you would for a group of trainees. This will help you get the "bugs" out of the program.

Problems that don't show up as you go through the training portion of the program will show up when you begin evaluating the effectiveness of the program.

## Conduct Program

The preparation and planning all come to fruition as you conduct your session. A pilot run or rehearsal will give you added confidence and, as a result of the constructive criticism of a trial audience, will help polish your teaching effort.

In planning a favorable learning climate, the trainees are induced to pay attention and take responsibility for learning. A favorable learning climate maximizes learning by offering the trainees a reason to learn, preparing them for the content of the training, and developing their trust in the instructor.

The following activities have been tested in numerous meetings and training sessions. These activities have been found successful in evoking participation from trainees and other meeting participants. They are:

*Develop a benefit list.* After a brief explanation of what the training is going to cover and how you are going to conduct the training session, ask the participants to think of the benefits that they will personally derive from the training. You can record their comments on a flipchart. Usually, they will fill the chart within four or five minutes.

With the benefits listed on a chart, all the participants can see and firmly establish in their own minds the value they will get from the training. The fact that the group developed the list, rather than the instructor, gives it added validity. Generally the trainees are motivated to receive the training so they may realize the listed benefits.

*Conduct a discussion period.* A discussion period serves two useful functions. First, it keeps the participants interested and involved in the learning activity, and second, it gives them an opportunity to fulfill their personal needs for expression. During the discussion period, participants can socialize and relieve any tension that may have built up during the time they were listening to the trainer.

*Design activities to promote participation.* You can ensure the involvement of everyone by designing your activities for small groups. You might have four or five people in a group and have a specific function assigned to each group member. Every member must then participate in order for the group to perform its function.

Another way to ensure participation is to provide freedom to make mistakes. Most people who are reluctant to participate in group activities are reluctant because they fear they will be ridiculed for making mistakes. You can eliminate this feeling by explaining that making mistakes is simply one of the ways we learn. Once the group accepts this, the reluctance to participate will end.

### Evaluate Program

Although evaluation is an ongoing process, end-of-course formal evaluation should be a part of every program. Evaluation can take any of several forms, for example, tests, on-the-job performance, superior-subordinate reports, and behavior or performance changes and results. Rating sheets by participants can be helpful if they are properly constructed. Informal evaluation and observation should be continuous.

Evaluation is an educational feedback system that measures the effectiveness of our actions. We use it to learn and correct our errors. In training, you can preselect evaluation criteria by relating to the specific objectives that you established for the program.

For example, if your objective was to get new information across, then your evaluation criteria will relate to the level of information understood and retained by the trainee. If your objective was to develop new skills, your evaluation must relate to skill acquisition. Your criteria for evaluation represent an evaluation of the specificity of the objective you developed. If the objectives were not specific and measurable, the deficiency will show up in your attempt to develop evaluation criteria.

### Revise Program

Tomorrow's session will always be better if we learn to accept constructive suggestions from our peers, our superiors, and our participants. Perhaps too much (or too little) time was spent on one session. If our goals were not satisfactorily attained, major revision is in order. If goals were reached and the evaluative response and results were favorable, it is still good advice to review and revise bits and pieces.

### SUMMARY

Training needs must be carefully researched before a training program is designed. You can begin to realize that an effective training program doesn't "just happen." Like anything of value, it is deliberately and painstakingly constructed from start to finish—and from the finish line back to the starting point! A well-designed training program is an integrated collection of knowledge, skills, and attitudes, all carefully blended to mold a specific product—the desired learning under specified conditions. While the approach may appear cumbersome and arduous (as indeed it may be), the dividends returned for the expenditure of time and effort are well worth it! Like an artist proud of his or her latest canvas, so, too, can you be equally proud of your carefully drawn and designed training program.

# CHAPTER 3

# Determining Training Needs

*Training won't solve all problems.*
*Not all problems are training problems.*

The novice trainer is well advised to remember these two statements. Ambitious practitioners, anxious to make their presence known to new employers, may be prone to suggest training as the panacea for all the organization's ills. Usually, however, this is not the case.

Training programs should be offered as a response to a need, not merely as a quick, sure-fire solution to a given problem. It may well be that the solutions to these problems may be found in the area of personnel, product, promotion, or production. These, and a host of other factors, should be explored before embarking on the training program.

## BASIC TRAINING AREAS

The three basic areas involved in performance are the generally accepted types of learning: cognitive (knowledge), psychomotor (skills), and affective (attitudes).

A person must have the basic conceptual knowledge of what is to be done on the job, the rationale for the job, and what the results of doing the job will be. Cognitive understanding of how to perform the job is equally important.

The second basic area, the skills or psychomotor area, relates to motor or manual skills. This area includes specific physical movements and actions that people take in the performance of their jobs. Often trainers can play an important role in increasing productivity through training activities that shorten the number of movements and actions or that establish new move-

Psychomotor

Domains of learning

ments that are more productive than the old ones. Work simplification programs, for example, continually attempt to find a "better way."

The third basic area, the attitudinal area (affective domain), is as important as the first two. This important area is often overlooked because the research design does not investigate it. Research has shown that poor employee attitudes have serious effects on productivity. Employees who feel that they are being treated unfairly, that their work is unimportant, or that they are in a hopeless situation, work far below their level of capability.

The productivity crisis of the early 1980s brought this to light in an emphatic way. While there were several causal factors of America's productivity problems, management's disregard for the changing work force was a key factor. A younger, better educated employee, coupled with the growing number of women entering the world of work, found many organizations uncertain as to how to handle this "new breed." Consequently, worker dissatisfaction and a resultant decrease in productivity plagued a number of companies.

## DETERMINING TRAINING NEEDS

Often training is approached on a hit-and-miss basis. We pick out a skills (psychomotor) program for one year, an attitudinal (affective) program for the next year, and, perhaps, a general knowledge (cognitive) program for another year. Unfortunately, these programs may not relate to the real needs of the organization. We may be training production people to improve quality while the more pressing need may be to improve the selling skills of the sales force.

Sometimes the need for training may be perceived incorrectly. For example, a sales manager may feel that the sales representatives need product knowledge training, while an analysis of the situation may reveal that the sales personnel need the skills to *present* the product rather than additional knowledge about the product. Here is where a systematic procedure for determining the needs of the organization is required.

## WHY DO NEEDS ANALYSIS?

Before we enumerate several ways to conduct a needs analysis, it might be instructive to suggest some reasons for spending the time and effort in the first place.

Initially, a study of the work environment and the personnel involved will identify the existing level of employee performance. Measured against industry standards, we could compare manufacturing output, for example, to other similar product lines. In office situations where productivity is admittedly difficult to measure, other areas of need might surface. As an illustration, a personality conflict between clerical employees may turn up as the culprit. A program on conflict resolution could address that issue.

Second, a needs analysis could target individuals who most need additional training or development. Through interviews, for example, a person may request assistance in a refresher course for a present job. Or, perhaps, a supervisor may suggest individuals to attend a program for new skills needed for a promotion. Through a variety of methods, people can be identified who can materially benefit from additional learning opportunities.

Third, a needs analysis is an excellent vehicle to get a pulse of what the organization is all about. It can provide management with the prevailing attitude or morale of the employees. Administering carefully constructed questionnaires, to be completed anonymously, can often encourage employees to "tell it like it is."

Fourth, a needs analysis reveals information about the organizational climate. Learning about employee attitudes and conducting needs surveys can help us to get a picture of the total organization. Pinpointing certain weaknesses may alert the astute researcher to an impending dangerous situation. Conversely, a productive team effort in a well-managed organization is also revealed by a needs analysis.

Fifth, a needs analysis involves the entire work force. People often appreciate being asked their opinions. Of the several methods discussed, many actually involve the individual employee. Would-be participants have a hand, therefore, in helping to design the training effort. Their comments, feelings, or opinions about given content areas may help you construct your training effort.

Finally, because it involves employees and management, these same people feel they have played a part in designing the program. After all, the best training programs are based on identified needs. Therefore, they become "a part of" instead of "a part from" the program.

## Types of Needs Analysis

A determination of training needs can run the spectrum from a simple question ("What do you think 'we need most?") to a complex research design. Some of the more commonly used types of analysis include:

- Informal interview
- Observation
- Survey method
- Performance tests
- Formal interviews
- Reports from superiors
- Examination of records
- Advisory committees
- Checklists
- Assessment centers
- Questionnaires
- Management requests
- Formal research

Let's examine each of these in some detail.

*Informal interview.* As suggested by its title, this technique can be easily accomplished without a great deal of research or background. It could take place over a cup of coffee or during a casual lunchtime conversation. You should be cautioned, of course, about not appearing to be prying or playing a clandestine role. If the conversation is initiated by the potential recipient group, so much the better. If not, tactful questioning must be used to ferret out the real training problem.

*Observation.* Equally informally, the trainer can discover areas of potential training needs through observational methods. For example, an overheard misunderstanding between employees may indicate a need for communications or human relations training. A complaint from a coworker about outgoing correspondence may indicate a need for some clerical training. Don't assume, however, that what you may sense as a training need is always—and solely—a training need. You may see only the surface of the problem or you may even misread the entire picture.

*Survey method.* Questionnaires are typically constructed to determine the types of training needed. Since it is often too costly or time-consuming to poll all the personnel in your organization, you may randomly select certain groupings that are deemed representative of the department or organization. In constructing a questionnaire, have a pilot group critique the instrument for clarity or ambiguity. If supervisory clearance is required, you should ask your superiors to also assist in the critique before you administer the survey to the chosen group.

*Performance tests.* The achievement level of individuals and groups can be assessed through testing. Entry-level skills, for example, are easily measured. After a person has been on the job for a time, periodic appraisal may show a real need for cognition, affective, or even psychomotor updating. Commercial tests on a variety of content areas are readily available should internal sources be lacking.

*Formal interviews.* Personal interviews with employees may uncover a wide scope of training needs. To preclude any "backwash" or negative feedback from the interviewee's superior, it is always necessary to respect the confidentiality of the responses. Problems seen on the job may be traced to an ineffective or inhuman manager. Delicacy in handling these incidents is extremely important. If the interview is conducted by the manager of that respective department, you will seldom find the frank and candid responses given to a third party if anonymity is ensured.

*Reports from superiors.* These requests may come from an individual's superior or from an official of the organization. In the latter, of course, you are advised to take prompt action, but remember that the request may not be a bona fide training need. Again, an honest inquiry on your part may articulate the real problem or dispose of an artificial one.

Supervisors are becoming increasingly people oriented and can be a sincere and continuing source of information regarding areas where training is needed. We must realize that people don't always know what they need or may mistakenly cite an incorrect need.

*Records examination.* A variety of needs may be uncovered by reviewing employee efficiency and production records. A quick check with your personnel department will determine which records may be available. Since laws are becoming more stringent, be certain you are not checking on information considered to be privileged data.

Assuming these records are approved for your perusal, several areas of need may be brought to your attention. Productivity, sales, operating ratios, and so on are but a few of the items that may be compared to pinpoint an individual need.

*Advisory committees.* Every organization should have a training committee composed of several individuals representing key departments or agencies of that organization. Monthly or periodic meetings of this group serve as a "sounding board" for new program ideas, and each committee member functions as a representative of his or her respective department. Training requests could be funneled through that person and brought to the committee for disposition. If possible, your committee should have members from all levels of the organization (employee, supervisory, middle management, and top management). This group can be your best friend in your training efforts. Use it wisely.

*Checklists.* A simple checklist can be administered and tabulated with a minimum of effort. Figures 3-1 and 3-2 show two forms that can be adapted to meet the needs of most organizations. Respondents merely indicate their areas of interest or concern. A tally is then easily compiled.

*Assessment centers.* Though time-consuming and elaborate, the use of assessment centers can pinpoint an individual's need for improvement. Essentially, an assessment center is the site of a carefully controlled process where skilled observers evaluate the behaviors and actions of participants. Assessment centers are used primarily in middle- and upper-management circles.

*Questionnaires.* Another excellent vehicle, the questionnaire can provide significant amounts of critical information. Attitude surveys often take this form. Typically, these surveys cover attitudes, reactions, and feelings about satisfaction (or lack thereof) with the organization, industry, job, or work itself. Working conditions, pay or salary, supervisors, coworkers, and a host of relevant issues may also be investigated.

*Management requests.* There may be times when key management personnel suggest that certain topics or programs be considered. The perspective they bring is of particular interest since quick follow-up and carry-through is of obvious importance. Their requests may be for members of top management or for subordinates in respective areas of the organization. Regardless of the source, we are well advised to treat these requests as valued training needs. In those rare cases, however, where such a request is somewhat afield of a definitive training program, consult with your own immediate superior or seek advice from your training committee.

*Formal research.* Your internal research should be directed at eliminating the discrepancy between actual and perceived needs. You can do this by developing evidence that clearly demonstrates what the real need is and presenting this evidence in a way that shows how the perceived need will be fulfilled by the training program. You can accomplish these goals by concentrating your research on training's relationship to the actual problem.

**Figure 3-1.** Survey of Supervisory Training Needs

NAME _____

BUREAU _____

PLEASE INDICATE YOUR LEVEL OF SUPERVISORY RESPONSIBILITY BY CHECKING ONE OF THE FOLLOWING:

☐ first-line supervisor (the employees you supervise do not supervise others)
☐ second-line supervisor (you supervise employees who also have supervisory responsibilities)
☐ management level

I. PLEASE INDICATE BY CHECKING THE APPROPRIATE COLUMN THE DEGREE OF NEED YOU THINK EXISTS FOR TRAINING FIRST-LINE SUPERVISORS ONLY.

| | GREAT NEED | SOME NEED | LITTLE NEED |
|---|---|---|---|
| 1. COMMUNICATIONS | | | |
| 2. INTERVIEWING | | | |
| 3. COUNSELING | | | |
| 4. DISCIPLINING | | | |
| 5. HIRING PROCEDURES | | | |
| 6. TERMINATION PROCEDURES | | | |
| 7. DEVELOPING EMPLOYEES | | | |
| 8. MOTIVATING | | | |
| 9. HUMAN RELATIONS | | | |
| 10. HANDLING COMPLAINTS/GRIEVANCES | | | |
| 11. PLANNING/ORGANIZING | | | |
| 12. PERFORMANCE APPRAISAL | | | |
| 13. DECISION MAKING | | | |
| 14. LEADERSHIP | | | |
| 15. FUNCTIONING IN THE ORGANIZATION | | | |
| 16. DELEGATION | | | |
| 17. MANAGEMENT METHODS (e.g., M.B.O.) | | | |
| 18. BUDGETING | | | |
| 19. TIME MANAGEMENT | | | |
| 20. CONDUCTING MEETINGS | | | |
| 21. REPORTING SYSTEMS (written information) | | | |
| 22. SAFETY (e.g., Osha, First aid) | | | |
| 23. AFFIRMATIVE ACTION/E.E.O. | | | |

II. PLEASE INDICATE ANY OTHER SUPERVISORY SKILLS FOR WHICH YOU FEEL THERE MAY BE A NEED. LIST THEM BELOW AND CHECK THE APPROPRIATE BOX INDICATING THE DEGREE OF NEED.

| | GREAT NEED | SOME NEED | LITTLE NEED |
|---|---|---|---|
| 1. | | | |
| 2. | | | |
| 3. | | | |
| 4. | | | |
| 5. | | | |

26

**Figure 3-2.** Needs

Listed below are statements describing the needs of supervisors and/or managers. In the box preceding each, place the number 3, 2, 1, to indicate the degree to which they apply to your population. Here's the code:

**3 = highly applicable, extremely important.**
**2 = moderately applicable, fairly important.**
**1 = slight or no applicability, not too relevant here.**

☐ ability to set realistic goals or standards, define performance requirements, and develop action plans for achieving and for controlling (tracking) performance.

☐ skill in communicating effectively in face-to-face situations—with subordinates, peers, superiors, customers, etc.

☐ commitment to Theory Y management, willingness to delegate and develop subordinates to their fullest.

☐ skill in balancing their daily activities between the demands of the task (production-oriented side) and of the employees (people-oriented side).

☐ ability to apply motivation theory so as to increase job satisfaction and to develop a team of "turned on" employees.

☐ skill in giving on-the-job training and counseling relating to behavior at work.

☐ ability to appraise performance objectively and to conduct regular, constructive performance reviews that are two-way dialogues.

☐ sensitivity to the needs, interests, goals, and perceptions of others through transactional analysis.

☐ skill in writing letters, memos, and reports that are clear, concise, complete, and compelling . . . writing that gets action.

☐ ability to manage time (of self and others) effectively by prioritizing, controlling interruptions, measuring cost effectiveness of time invested, etc.

☐ skill in cutting costs through methods improvement, work simplification or reallocation, flow charting, analysis of procedures, etc.

☐ ability to hold meetings, briefings, and conferences that are well organized, crisp, and produce results.

☐ skill in negotiating and resolving conflict as it arises in interpersonal relations.

☐ facility in listening in depth, drawing out what is and isn't said, summarizing and clarifying, and organizing the speaker's message so that it can be acted upon.

☐ ability to identify problems (separating causes from symptoms), to evaluate evidence, to weigh alternatives, and to select appropriate solution paths.

☐ skill in implementing management by objectives at the departmental level (preparing action plans, performance documents, etc.).

☐ knowledge of the laws and their role in making EEO and your affirmative action plan a reality in their work groups.

In the space below, please enter any other needs that are not covered above but are important to your population of supervisors and/or managers: _____

_____

_____

You should prepare your research guideline in such a way that only pertinent information is collected. There are a multiplicity of training needs in the minds of people at any given time. These needs may (or may not) apply to the problem at hand. If you are making a general survey to determine a wide range of needs throughout the organization, then you should use a very open questioning technique. When dealing with a performance problem, however, a questioning technique that will restrict the answers to needs associated with performance deficiencies is necessary. The following four steps will help you achieve that purpose:

1. Write a statement of the perceived training need and the expected result of that training as expressed in the training request.

2. Write a statement of the problem and the primary causes of the problem as determined by the problem analysis (described in Chapter 1).

3. State the discrepancy existing between current performance and the desired performance.

4. Develop your research questions to determine what training is needed, and by whom, to eliminate the performance deficiencies. Separate the components of knowledge, skills, and attitudes.

### Internal Research Sources

After you have constructed your research questions, the next step is to start collecting data. Whether you are interviewing, observing, or examining records, your activities will be directed by your research questions. All collected data should be identified as to their source and the questions to which they relate. This identification will help you weigh the importance of each response when you tabulate your results.

Each research project may require different sources of information. For one problem you may be required to examine several sources of information, while another will require only one or two sources. The following sources are also useful in research:

- Activity records covering current and previous results

- Supervisory evaluations of subordinate performance

- Job descriptions or task analysis reports

- Written policies and procedures applicable to the situation

- Activity records of similar departments

- Personnel evaluations, including employee tests and questionnaire results

- The tools, equipment, and supplies being used to do the job

- Interviews with the supervisors of the target group

- Interviews with the target group

- Interviews with other groups who interact with the target group

Once you have completed your internal research and tabulated your data, you must analyze the data to determine whether or not training will do the job and what types of training need to be done. The following questions will be helpful in making this analysis:

- If the actual need is part of a problem, will training solve the problem?

- If a behavioral change is required, can training effect this change?

- What specific people need the training?

- Will the new behavior be reinforced on the job?

- Can the training program and the expected results be evaluated?

- Will training fulfill the perceived needs and generate the expected performance results expressed in the training request?

Once the needs are definitively established, you will find these procedures useful in setting forth your plan:

- State, in writing, the need that the training program is designed to fill.

- Indicate the method that will be used to evaluate the result.

- Establish the minimum acceptable level of proficiency the trainee must achieve.

- Describe the stages of growth the trainee will go through.

- Delineate the various levels of proficiency attributable to each stage of growth.

- Describe the expected skill development or change on the job, after training.

- Spell out the value system constraints and supports of the group who will receive the training.

- Define the communication network:
  a) Data collection and storage
  b) Self-correcting criteria
  c) Retrieval
  d) Utilization

- Describe the executive or organizational support.

- Indicate the rewards likely to accrue to the successful participant.

## THE TRAINING PROPOSAL

Once a needs analysis has been completed, you are ready to prepare a training proposal. This assumes, of course, that the analysis indicated a need for training. If the needs analysis indicated a performance deficiency, for example, then the objective of the training proposal will be to remove the deficiency through training. The proposal should spell out the need for training, the expected results, the people to be trained, and the expected consequences if training is not conducted, and it should include an outline of the proposed program. The following sample proposal covers these points.

### Sample Proposal

INTERCOMPANY MEMO
FROM:     JOHN PLACER, DIRECTOR OF TRAINING
TO:         GEORGE GROWLER, V. P. OPERATIONS
SUBJECT: TRAINING PROPOSAL

*Objective*
Reduce costs of "widget" stampings by 10 percent.

*The Need for Training*
A needs analysis was conducted in the production department to determine if training could improve performance and lower production costs. Our analysis indicated that two major problems can be reduced by training. One is the abnormally high waste factor, found to be 14 percent of stamping stock, and the second is the improper handling procedures being followed by the stock feeders.

Sheet steel stock is being damaged in the warehouse and on the line. This damage due to improper handling is a major cause of the high waste factor. Waste is also occurring due to improper alignment procedures by the stock feeder.

*Expected Results*
Proper handling and feeding procedures should result in the waste factor being lowered to approximately 4 percent. About 7 percent of the reduction will accrue from improved handling procedures and 3 percent from improved stock feeding procedures.

*Prospects for Training*
All lift-truck operators and stock clerks in the sheet steel warehouse and all stamping machine operators and feeders should be trained. Currently, there are fourteen machine operators, fourteen feeders, six lift-truck operators, and two stock clerks. The thirty-six prospective trainees should be trained concurrently to gain the support of all those involved.

*Outline of the Program*

## WASTE REDUCTION TRAINING PROGRAM

I. Orientation
   a) Explain problem and training objective to participants.
   b) Establish minimum level of proficiency trainees must achieve.
   c) Explain rewards or benefits participants will receive by reaching required proficiency level.

II. Concurrent training sessions in warehouse and in production department
   a) Demonstration
   b) Practice session
   c) On-the-job test

III. Discussion
   a) Problems encountered
   b) Suggested solutions

IV. Second session
   a) Demonstration
   b) Practice session
   c) On-the-job test

V. Evaluation
   a) Waste factor results
   b) Performance results
   c) Attitude results

*Expected Conditions without Training*
Without training, the waste factor is expected to continue at the current 14 percent waste level. This level may even increase as the cumulative effect of poor attitudes and improper work habits reinforce each other over time.

*Recommendations*
A training program is recommended to begin immediately and is expected to last approximately three months, with follow-up tests and evaluation to continue for one year.

## SUMMARY

As you can now readily attest, needs assessment can be as basic or as sophisticated as one wants it to be. Is it really worth all the time and trouble?

Yes! Properly done, a needs analysis offers a systematic appraisal of training and development. While the 3 *R*s may be satisfactory for the primary school, the major focus in the work place is the 3 *P*s—people, performance, and productivity.

Needs analysis can find answers to these important questions:

Is the training needed?

Who needs it?

What are their needs?

Are they aware of their needs?

What topics should be covered?

How soon should the training be held?

These are just a few of the items that require attention. With a thoughtful and deliberate evaluation of the wants and needs identified, training objectives can be defined and a productive and viable training program planned.

# CHAPTER 4

# Instructional Objectives

*You can't get lost if you don't know where you're going.*

In planning any kind of a road trip, common sense dictates that we initially search out our destination and then plot backward to our starting point. When we're ready for the trip, we already have identified our objective as the destination point. Depending on the length of the journey, we may have also defined some subgoals or stopover points along the way.

It is wise to do similar planning for every training effort in which you are engaged. And yet, as startling as it may seem, far too many training programs are started every day with little if any idea as to what the end goal or objective might be.

It's been said that you can never be lost if you don't really know where you're going! While that may be true, it's a sorry state to be in when it comes to human resource development.

It is incumbent on each of us to know precisely what the end product or training objective of each session and program is before the training actually starts. It is equally important for the participants to recognize that we have defined goals toward which we are all driving. Only then can we have a fruitful and rewarding journey.

## GOALS AND OBJECTIVES

The terms *goals* and *objectives* are often used interchangeably. One dictionary definition states:

> goal: an end or objective
> objective: something worked toward or striven for: a goal

For our purposes, however, we have elected to differentiate between these terms. We suggest that a training goal be a *general* statement of what the training is intended to accomplish.

A training objective is a *specific* statement or change in the knowledge, skills, or attitudinal areas.

## PROGRAMMING TRAINING OBJECTIVES

If we design every aspect of a training program with evaluation in mind, we must program training objectives that specify behavioral change leading directly to the accomplishment of specific organizational goals. In writing objectives, keep in mind that the behavioral change required to obtain these results must be reinforced if the behavior is to continue in the actual work situation. Behavior that is learned in the artificial situation of a classroom will seldom be carried over to the job unless that new behavior is rewarded on the job.

In this chapter, we discuss behavioral objectives and the variables that affect the success of your training program. Both short-term and long-term objectives are considered in relation to the training approach required for each. You will be given specific guidelines for developing each type of training program.

You will also learn how to test your objectives against criteria that will ensure the success of the program. You will be given ways to test the written materials for clarity and a checklist to use in determining the effectiveness of the design of your written program. You will also see how to demonstrate the program's credibility and its value to the organization.

## PREPARING INSTRUCTIONAL OBJECTIVES

Instructional objectives must delimit the training activities to those that lead to the achievement of specific results. The overriding goal, then, becomes the change in performance that will be required to reach training or organizational goals. The training objective will be to provide the skills, knowledge, or attitude improvement that will result in the attainment of the specified goals. This criterion provides the basis for later evaluation of the results of training.

### Short-term Operational Objectives

Short-term objectives are those that are associated with "first-level training." For example, it might be the training required to develop employees to the point where they can operate a machine, go through the basic steps of the job assignment, and be generally aware of what is required in the performance of those duties. The first level is thought of as the apprentice or trainer level.

Short-term objectives are also related to *ad hoc* programs for new employee indoctrination, special informational programs, and new policies or procedures. Once an *ad hoc* workshop or lecture is completed, the program is discarded or filed until a similar situation arises again.

**First-level Skills Objectives** A program covering first-level skills provides detailed job knowledge and the correct procedures for accomplishing the job tasks. Learning objectives should contain progression steps that permit the employee to change an attitude, knowledge, or skill on a step-by-step basis. The behavioral change that is expected to take place at each step should be written into the objective so that it may be evaluated.

Management expectation for performance should be considered in determining the objectives. The expected "how and when" should be set up as guidelines, but flexibility should be maintained to allow for differences in the trainees' individual learning rates.

The objectives should specify short-range levels of proficiency that are acceptable for each step. The particular training method—lecture, programmed instruction, or on-the-job coaching—should be spelled out for each phase in the program. Obviously, the various steps may require different methods of instruction.

It is important to establish an information system to support the trainees from the very beginning. The trainees need to know who is responsible for the many functions related to the job. Detailed instructions on what to do or where to go when equipment, space, or policy is interfering with the accomplishment of their tasks should be explained.

**Special Program Objectives** Often the training department is required to prepare special programs for a specific purpose. There may be a special problem to solve, a policy to implement, temporary assignments to prepare people for an organizational change, or perhaps a move to a new location. Training personnel are often termed "change agents" and are specially skilled in preparing guidelines for these kinds of organizational change. The objective for such special programs might be the development of a guideline to be followed in making the required change.

The following adaptation of a problem-solving technique should help you in developing guidelines for special programs:

1. Diagnose the problem or objective:

   a) List the causes of the problem or obstacles that may interfere with achieving the objective.

    b) Pick the most significant obstacle or cause and develop it into a written statement of a program objective.

    c) List the subproblems that must be resolved.

2. Reduce the written objective into specific terms:

    a) State the specific purpose to be accomplished and the time frame.

    b) State the specific skill to be learned or the specific methods to be used in accomplishing the purpose.

3. Establish evaluation criteria:

    a) List the required levels of proficiency.

    b) List the indirect resources or other people who will be needed or whose actions will affect the results.

    c) Restate the written objective, considering the evaluation criteria.

4. Develop a step-by-step guideline for reaching the objective:

    a) List as many possible solutions as you can think up.

    b) Write a brief evaluation for each solution.

    c) Select and write out, for use in your guideline, the solution most likely to succeed.

The guideline, of course, will have to take into account the attitudes, skills, and knowledge required for each step. Also, consideration must be given to the subproblems in 1–c. Often a solution generated for the main problem objective will also solve the subproblems. If not, the subproblems must be solved in the same manner as the main problem.

### Long-term Comprehensive Objectives

Long-term training objectives are directed at second-level or professional development. These improvements in proficiency occur over a long period of time and are affected by the employees' attitudes as well as their knowledge and skills. Comprehensive objectives must be based on an awareness of the part these attitudes, knowledge, and skills play in employee development.

Proficiency develops over a long period of time but occurs in small increments or improvement steps. Training must be designed so that it relates to the particular stage of development the employees are experiencing. The training objectives should be related to the employees' long-range attempts to reach their potential and to the long-range goals of the organization.

The attitudes, knowledge, and skills necessary for the attainment of the long-range goals of the organization are all part of the trainer's objectives in training people to perform their jobs. Feedback and reinforcement are necessary to guide the employees' attempts at improvement. Since employees are going through various stages of training throughout their career, the training objectives must harmonize with the feedback and support system in the work place. If employees are trained to behave one way but rewarded for performing differently, they will learn to perform differently. Management commitment should be secured for the training program as well as a reinforcement system for the learned behavior.

## BEHAVIORAL OBJECTIVES

Robert Mager, a prolific writer and respected voice in human resource development, sent the training world back to its drawing board several years ago when he challenged us to think in behavioral terms. Far too many of our academic and training colleagues confuse the terms *purpose, goal,* and *objectives.* His thoughtful and continuing contributions have made his name synonymous with behavioral objectives.

One of the most significant steps, then, in human resource development is that of defining objectives in behavioral terms. Too many training programs are obscure as to their purpose; too many training sessions are unclear as to their specific objectives.

An objective is stated in behavioral terms when the trainer can demonstrate the material learned in an observable way. For example, if at the end of the secretarial training, the learner is to demonstrate proficiency by being able to type sixty words a minute with 95 percent accuracy in a two-minute timed test, then that objective is stated behaviorally.

It is imperative that the end result of training be both measurable and observable.

Behavioral objectives can help determine the content of the program. As a solid basis for evaluation, they provide an excellent opportunity for both trainee and trainer to determine accurately the achievement level reached.

Writing behavioral objectives is a difficult task. It is made easier if you remember to answer these questions:

Who will perform the task?

What will be measured?

What is the minimum level of performance?

How is the task evaluated?

The wording of objectives is critical. Many verbs we so often see used are not acceptable. For example:

"To understand . . ."

"To appreciate . . ."

"To know . . ."

"To recognize . . ."

The problem with these words is one of interpretation. It is difficult to measure understanding or appreciation. How do you know that the learners have achieved an understanding? How can we possibly determine when our trainees or participants have satisfactorily achieved a satisfaction? You can readily see the problem. We have no way of knowing when the objective is attained or mastered.

More specific verbs include:

"To write . . ."

"To construct . . ."

"To assemble . . ."

"To identify . . ."

"To adjust . . ."

"To measure . . ."

"To solve . . ."

As is readily seen, these are action verbs and are easily measured. Mager's publication entitled *Preparing Instructional Objectives* made an outstanding contribution to human resource development. Three basic concepts form the foundation for his work:

- *Behavior:* any overt or visible activity displayed or performed by the learner

- *Terminal behavior:* the behavior the trainer demonstrates at the conclusion of the training effort

- *Criterion:* the standard or test by which we measure or evaluate the behavior

Let's look at a few examples to help us understand these concepts. For example, the objective is: "Given a one-hour exam of one hundred multiple-choice questions, the trainee will attain a score of at least 75 percent." Clearly, the three basic tests have been met.

Try this one. "The trainee will understand the basic workings of the Model 2745 Engine." Has this objective been stated in behavioral terms?

No. "Understand" is not acceptable, and the criterion test cannot be measured or evaluated because it is stated in nebulous terms.

"At the conclusion of this training session, the learner will be able to fill out completely our Form 2714 with no errors." The specificity of the terminal behavior can be easily measured.

One more: ". . . to really understand and appreciate the principles of management." If you said no, you're well on the way to a better knowledge of Mager's principles.

## TASK ANALYSIS

To make course objectives more meaningful, first construct a task analysis. As its name implies, this activity is a detailed, intricate method for actually isolating and studying the many component parts of any job. It is a method for describing a procedural job as a basis for preparing instructional materials. It forces the writer to break down the task into its most elemental and simple components. The activity can then be described in easy-to-understand parts.

Here is a process you can use for writing a task analysis:

1. Prepare a card for each element of the task.

    a) Preceding condition (stimulus).

    b) Imperative verb describing action to be taken.

    c) Time, observation, and preparation for next step.

2. Justify the procedure: explain reason.

3. Arrange cards in sequential order linearly or in branching sequence.

    a) Linear sequence: each step follows the other without any alternatives.

    b) Branching sequence: steps are branched where discriminations or decisions are to be made.

4. Lay out the cards.

    a) Place a discrimination card to the right of the previous base card.

    b) Place a linear card below the previous base card.

    c) Make sure the last card in either direction advises readers that the sequence is ended or sends them to the next step.

5. Write the task instructions.

6. Use the card layout to form the major headings, subheadings, and discrimination headings.

7. Evaluate the analysis: let the trainee try it.

# Instructional Objectives

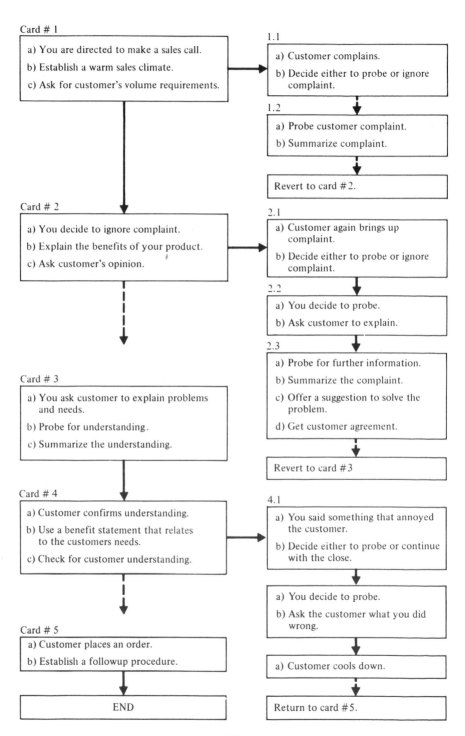

**Card # 1**

a) You are directed to make a sales call.

b) Establish a warm sales climate.

c) Ask for customer's volume requirements.

**1.1**

a) Customer complains.

b) Decide either to probe or ignore complaint.

**1.2**

a) Probe customer complaint.

b) Summarize complaint.

Revert to card #2.

**Card # 2**

a) You decide to ignore complaint.

b) Explain the benefits of your product.

c) Ask customer's opinion.

**2.1**

a) Customer again brings up complaint.

b) Decide either to probe or ignore complaint.

**2.2**

a) You decide to probe.

b) Ask customer to explain.

**2.3**

a) Probe for further information.

b) Summarize the complaint.

c) Offer a suggestion to solve the problem.

d) Get customer agreement.

Revert to card #3

**Card # 3**

a) You ask customer to explain problems and needs.

b) Probe for understanding.

c) Summarize the understanding.

**Card # 4**

a) Customer confirms understanding.

b) Use a benefit statement that relates to the customers needs.

c) Check for customer understanding.

**4.1**

a) You said something that annoyed the customer.

b) Decide either to probe or continue with the close.

a) You decide to probe.

b) Ask the customer what you did wrong.

a) Customer cools down.

**Card # 5**

a) Customer places an order.

b) Establish a followup procedure.

END

Return to card #5.

40

8. When the trainee commits an error, clarify the instructions.

9. Compare the trainer's performance with the objectives of the program.

A sample task-analysis-based card layout of a sales presentation is presented on page 40.

## SUMMARY

A goal or objective that is stated in broad, general terms is really not all that useful to either trainer or trainee. Properly constructed, a general goal gives the "big picture" or end result of a training effort.

Too often, we still see vague statements such as "to give managers an appreciation of the value of human relations," or some other shallow goal. To be useful, the specific ingredients of behavioral objectives must give clarity and purpose. Because they are measurable and observable, it can easily be determined if they are meeting their stated purpose. Admittedly, writing such an objective is no easy task. But its payoff in results makes the investment a profitable one!

# CHAPTER 5

# Lesson Planning

*Plan your work; work your plan.*

This well-worn phrase still holds good advice for both the novice and the "pro" in conducting human resource programs.

While senior trainers may not agree on a particular format or model for lesson planning, they all agree on the necessity of having some kind of working papers. This chapter will suggest outlines for your consideration and offer some sound and workable ideas about how to construct a written lesson plan.

## WHAT IS A LESSON PLAN?

A lesson plan is simply a blueprint that identifies the basic 5 Ws (who, what, where, when, and why), with a few other items thrown in. It includes the audience (who), the topic and content (what), the location (where), the time frames (when), and the objectives (why).

While these are important elements, a good lesson plan also includes additional items such as those suggested in Figure 5-1.

## PROGRAM CONTENT—LESSON PLANNING

An important part of the preparation for your session lies in your lesson-planning effort. As suggested, a lesson plan can take any of several forms and is merely a guideline for you to follow in your presentation.

There are several good reasons for constructing a lesson plan for every session in which you are involved.

- The plan will help you stay on the proper track and lead you to your stated objectives.

- Properly written, your lesson plan will give the sequence and priorities of the topics you want to cover, providing a systematic and logical order of the knowledge, skills, or attitudes you will discuss.

**Figure 5-1.** Lesson Plan Development

**Lesson Plan Project**

Course _____  Instructor _____

Unit _____  Date _____

Objective:

Equipment/Tools:

Supplies:

References:

| Main Topic(s) | Teaching Points | Media |
|---|---|---|
| | | |

Discussion Questions:

Evaluation:

- By staying with your game plan, you have a better chance that your trainees will attain the prescribed goals.

- With a well-constructed format, you can have a sense of self-confidence in knowing that your session is planned in advance.

- If your session is one that is repeated in other groups, the preparation and planning you have undertaken can be easily used by another instructor in your absence.

### Preparing a Written Lesson Plan

Our purpose is to explain briefly the procedure for developing a simple lesson plan. The framework we wish to establish is one that encompasses the purpose, the subject matter, the work environment of the trainees, the research resources of the organization, and the skills of the trainer in application. Figure 5-2 provides a sample of a lesson plan cover page.

**Devise a Research Plan** You might wish to begin your research by jotting down some preliminary notes to establish the framework for the project. Many of these spontaneously developed ideas may be discarded later, but they help you zero in on the target. What at first may seem irrelevant may provide a guideline that will prevent later mistakes. Check all possible reference materials that may provide content ideas for you. These include textbooks, journals, trade or industry publications, internally produced materials, and, of course, colleagues and others in your field of interest.

**List Your Key Points** This initial development of ideas provides the key points for the lesson plan. After you have listed your initial ideas, structure your list by establishing the environmental constraints. The material you cover in the lesson plan must fit the environment the trainees work in. If not, it will be difficult for them to retain the new skills in the work situation.

List the variables that affect the trainees' performance and the key ideas that will strengthen these variables. If the employees are rewarded for volume, quality, or variety of design, then concentrate on these items in your list of key points. Use words that describe the trainees' environment and appeal to their personal desires.

List the productivity levels that would be acceptable as a result of the training. This contrast will provide the basis needed for evaluation. You can now go over your list and delete any ideas that do not fall within the productivity and environmental constraints that you have established. You may have additional constraints depending upon the particular problem you face.

Many experienced trainers begin this task with a writing pad and some quiet time, free from distractions or interruptions. Brainstorm all the possible

**Figure 5-2.** Lesson Plan

Organization: _____   Date: _____

Department: _____ Lesson Plan No. _____

Title of Lesson Plan: _____

Instructor(s): _____ Time Allocation: _____

_____

Trainees: _____

Where: _____

Training Objectives:

Classroom Requirements:

Training Aids and Equipment:

Trainee Supplies:

Trainee Handouts:

References:

Instructor:

ideas and points you can think of that have any relevance to the topic at hand. This initial effort is an all-inclusive one, so list as many ideas as you possibly can. As you later separate the "nice to know" from the "need to know," your job will be an easier one.

**Writing the Lesson Plan** Now you are ready to write. You'll want to blend all of your listings into an organized, logical, step-by-step presentation. Further, you will formulate an introduction, a body, and a close. The following guidelines will help you prepare the lesson plan so that it will interest trainees and motivate them to participate:

1. State the objectives of the training.

2. Indicate the benefits for the trainee.

3. List the functions that are to be performed.

4. Describe each function in detail.

5. Provide for cognitive, attitudinal, and skills development.

6. Identify the visual aids needed.

7. Describe an activity to utilize the skills.

8. Provide for practice of the new skills.

9. Provide for participative exercises in which the trainees apply the new skills to real problems of their own.

10. Provide for peer evaluation.

11. Provide time for discussion.

**Test the Plan in a Mock Setting** After your lesson plan has been completed, you're ready to go—almost. Remember, "The best laid plans. . . ." No matter how clear your program seems to you, the finished product may have some wording that will confuse the trainees. You can eliminate most of these errors by conducting a mock training session.

Ask other members of the training department or other people on the management team to go through a pilot training session to help you critique and strengthen the outline. Make sure they understand that the lesson plan is still in the preparation stage and that you are seeking their counsel and advice.

Figure 5-3 shows a completed page from a lesson plan on motivating employees.

**Figure 5-3a.** Lesson Plan, *page 1*

Organization: _ASTD Natl. Conference_____  Date: _May 23, 1985_____

Department: _Training Competencies_____  Lesson Plan No. _#1_____

Title of Lesson Plan: _"Adult Learning? You've Got To Be Kidding!"_____

Instructor(s): _Edward E. Scannell_____  Time Allocation: _90 minutes_____

Audience: _Relatively New Trainers_____

Where: _Anaheim (CA) Convention Center, Santa Ana Room_____

Training Objectives:
1. To contrast 3–4 concepts of pedagogy vs. andragogy.
2. To identify at least three theories of adult learning.
3. To demonstrate several applications of learning principles.
4. To differentiate the "All-Star" from the "Falling-Star" Trainer.
5. To list at least six traits of the All-Star Trainer.

Classroom Requirements: 350 chairs (see attached diagram)
   12' × 16' raised platform
   lectern

Training Aids and Equipment: Lavalier microphone
   Overhead projector
   16mm
   12' × 12' screen
   NOTE: Session will be videotaped by ASTD

Trainee Supplies: Pens and pencils

Trainee Handouts: "What Every Trainer Should Know About Training"
   "All-Star Trainer"
   "Seven Steps to Better Training"

References: Human Resource Development. 1st Edition (Donaldson-Scannell).
   Games Trainers Play. (Newstrom-Scannell).

**Figure 5-3b.** Lesson Plan, *page 2*

TOPIC _____ "ADULT LEARNING? . . ." Page 1

| TIME | CONTENT | NOTES | A.V. |
|---|---|---|---|
| 3:00 p.m. | I. Speaker Intro | See Data Sheet | |
| 3:02 p.m. | II. Introduction & Overview | Free Speech Story | Transparency #1 |
| | A. Game Plan | | |
| | B. Objectives<br>1. Pedagogy vs. Andragogy<br>2. Theories<br>3. "All-Star"<br>4. Practicality | | |
| 3:05 p.m. | III. Climate Setting<br>A. Your Goals Today | Group Activity<br>"Why Here?" | Transparency #2 |
| | B. Learning Can Be Fun | *Meet 3–4 new people | |
| | C. Quick Group Intros | | |
| | D. Feedback | *Call on 2–3 groups | |
| 3:10 p.m. | IV. Adult Learning | *Not "Spectator Sport" | |
| | A. Andragogy-Pedagogy<br>1. Resentment<br>2. Experience<br>3. Readiness<br>4. Problem-Centered | *Knowles<br><br>*Not Kids<br><br>*Fire Truck Story<br>*Real World | Transparency #3 |
| 3:15 p.m. | B. Domains<br>1. Cognitive<br>2. Psychomotor<br>3. Affective | *Motivation Story | Transparency #4 |
| 3:20 p.m. | C. Levels of Learning | *"Dumb Thing" Anecdote | Transparency #5 |
| | 1. Unc. Incmptnt. | *Dumb but don't know it | |
| | 2. Con. Incmptnt. | *Dumb but you know it! | |
| | 3. Con. Cmptnt. | *You know that you know | |
| | 4. Unc. Cmptnt. | *Expert, Habit, etc. | |
| | **Handout Sheet #1** | Introduce Muppet Clip | 16mm Projector Film Clip #1 |
| | D. Laws of Learning | | |
| | 1. Effect | *"People learn best . . ."<br>*Lord Chesterfield<br>*Group Activity (1 minute)<br>*Use of color | (Muppets)<br>(3 min., 20 sec.) |
| 3:55 p.m. | 2. Exercise | *John Dewey<br>*Learn by doing<br>*Hand-to-chin exercise | |

## MAKING THE TRAINING MORE EFFECTIVE

To make the session effective, you will want to establish a good learning climate to make the trainees feel comfortable. You can expand their comfort zone to include the new behavior you want them to try. The following five steps have been found to be effective in expanding trainee comfort zones for skills training sessions:

1. Present the material in small sequential steps.

2. Demonstrate each step.

3. Have the trainees practice one step at a time.

4. Demonstrate the correction of errors.

5. Have the trainees practice the total activity.

1. *Present the materials in small sequential steps.*

People can learn the most complicated material if it is presented in a deliberate and methodical manner. By learning in sequence they see the relationship of each step to the next. This forms the logic or reason for learning the new system. This small-step approach permits trainees to feel comfortable; they are not overwhelmed with a great number of things to do all at once.

Thus, trainees expand their comfort zone, one step at a time, as they incorporate each small change into their own personal style of learning. Remember our earlier example of learning to drive? No one would expect a person to begin learning to drive by speeding down the highway at fifty-five miles an hour. You would expect someone first to learn the techniques of starting, moving slowly forward, moving slowly backward, stopping, and parking. The trainee would progress slowly, step-by-step, until comfortable with fifty-five miles an hour. In an adult learning situation, if the adult doesn't feel comfortable, the motivation may be to reject the uncomfortable change.

2. *Demonstrate each step.*

Often people who do not understand the instructions will not ask for clarification. To overcome this problem, demonstrate each step and ask for discussion. The demonstration, of course, should be made to look as easy as possible. This convinces the trainees that they will be able to do it also, and again their comfort zone is widened to include the change.

3. *Have the trainees practice one step at a time.*

It is important to have the trainees practice each step immediately after the demonstration. At this point they have been convinced that they can do it. In order to give every trainee an opportunity to practice, break the class into small subgroups and let them help each other. Stress that everyone must master the first step before going to the next.

4. *Demonstrate the correction of errors.*

Keep a close watch for errors. Walk around during each activity and make a list of the errors that are being made. These errors may persist and interfere with the total program if not corrected. Analyze the errors to see if the instructions are not clear at a particular point. You can then correct the instructions, if necessary. Finally, without relating them to specific individuals, identify the errors and demonstrate how to correct them. Provide time for anyone who wishes to practice the correction to do so.

5. *Have the trainees practice the total activity.*

The trainees have slowly widened their comfort zone to include all the required steps in the new skill. They are now ready to perform the new skill by tying all the individual steps together. At this point, you should again demonstrate the skill as it should be performed.

Provide sufficient time for everyone to master the skill. Usually people become comfortable with a new behavior if they practice it three times. If you provide the opportunity for this practice, you may expect very few problems when the trainees attempt to use the new skill on the job.

## SUMMARY

The time and effort you invest in lesson planning is one that is guaranteed to pay off in high dividends. Like a cookbook, it should contain a listing of all the ingredients that must be blended together.

By reviewing the suggested forms shown in this chapter, ferret out the individual points and items that may fit your own instructional style. It matters *little* what your preference might be. It matters *much* that you "plan your work and you work your plan."

# CHAPTER 6

# Methods of Instruction

*There's madness in my method.*

Well, we really hope not, but it may drive one "mad" trying to answer the question "Which method is the most effective?"

In trying to answer this query, let's turn our attention to methodology. By exploring several of the more commonly used techniques and methods for training, you will be able to decide which method may be best for a given lesson. While several techniques are listed, it is important to recognize that you as the trainer should have a working knowledge of all of them. In some cases, one or two techniques will be preferable, depending upon the objectives of the session and the background and interest of the people involved.

What is the most effective method? There is no simple answer. To help you make your decision, though, let's discuss the pros and cons of each. Certainly, good trainers will have a variety of techniques in their repertoires. As trainers gain experience, they tend to favor one or two methods and then continue to use only those. "Because this one is easier," is a weak reason to select a method. Unfortunately, however, even senior trainers have fallen into that trap.

There are some important items to consider in choosing a particular method. Obviously, there is merit in picking one with which we feel comfortable. We should, of course, consider first the objectives of that particular session. How about cost? Time, of course, is also important. For example, while we know that discussion may be better for learning, it may be we simply cannot afford the extra time and must settle instead for the lecture method. The size of the group and type of room are also relevant considerations in choosing appropriate methods.

Here, then, are some commonly used methods.

## LECTURE

Without question, the lecture method is both the most widely used and the most abused technique of training. It is primarily a one-way communication: one person presents a prepared talk or a series of facts or information of a particular subject. The lecture is very economical in that little time is wasted with discussion. If it is properly prepared, the meaning of a message can be clearly stated and illustrated. Some of the prime advantages of the lecture include these items:

*Time-saving.* When there is a lot of material to present to a group, the lecture is often the best choice since it allows the entire group to be given the information in a relatively short period of time.

*Control of topic.* The trainer is in complete control of the session since all of the information is presented with little if any time for questions or feedback. This enables trainers with well-prepared lesson plans to gauge accurately the time elements of their presentations.

*Repetition.* Because the trainer is in such control of the meeting, points can easily be repeated for emphasis and clarification.

*Economy.* As suggested previously, the trainer can present a lot of new material to most any size group, thus saving time and talent. Assuming that the trainees are listening to the material being presented, it is easy to see that giving large groups the same information is an economical training method.

*Flexible group size.* The lecture is applicable to any size group. With appropriate audio and visual aids, the lecture can be used with large groups.

We must also consider the disadvantages of the lecture method:

*One-way communication.* Without some method of testing or evaluation, the trainer has little assurance that the message is really being understood or received properly. Because of a lack of participation, there is no feedback or no real reinforcement of the learning process.

*Boredom.* Too many trainers or teachers forget that a lack of variety of voice style and methodologies will undercut the effectiveness of the session. A dull, dreary monotone makes it extremely difficult for the trainee to listen to what is being presented.

*Attention span.* Most people listening to a lecture have an extremely limited span of attention. Studies indicate that immediately after hearing something, the average person will have forgotten 50 percent of that material! The lecturer must repeat and summarize frequently to overcome this drawback.

*Lower retention rate.* Because of a lack of involvement or participation, the lecture has a much lower rate of learning as measured by long- and short-term retention.

*The canned talk.* Too many trainers forget the individualization of their trainees and are too prone to "pull" a session out of the file drawer and merely redo it for that "new group." The canned talk is inherently boring and contributes to lack of attention on the part of the trainees. Listeners can quickly see through canned talks and hence they lose any value for the individual.

*Feedback.* Because of the one-way communication of the lecture, the speakers or trainers have no way of knowing whether they are staying on track or going completely afield in regard to the interests of the group. They may be expanding on a point that is of no interest whatever to their listeners; hence, the group loses all interest. Since the lack of feedback is an inherent disadvantage of the lecture, trainers must be assured that their content and presentation are such as to overcome this negative point.

A lecture is useful for presenting new material such as policy changes or general information that has not previously been available to the trainees. Questions are usually restricted to clarifying the lecture material. The main advantage of the lecture is speed.

## Lecture Discussion

The lecture discussion is a modified version of the lecture, combining the content session with some discussion on the part of the trainees. This easy modification helps to overcome some of the earlier disadvantages of the lecture technique used by itself.

A lecture can be improved by asking questions that make the audience think about your ideas or concepts. The following questions can be adapted to this purpose:

How does this compare with what you used to do?

What do you think the reason for this is?

What do you think the outcome will be?

What are the alternative methods that could be used?

A discussion allows individual participation even with large training programs. As implied by the term, discussion involves the people in either large or small group sessions to further comment on the training session at hand.

Discussion brings many views into play and brings out details required for understanding. By promoting a free exchange of ideas, the members take responsibility for learning. The purpose is to explore a subject and permit questioning that will bring out the unclear areas so they can be cleared up. The advantage of discussion is that you get immediate feedback and can, therefore, immediately correct any misunderstanding. One of the disadvantages is that the group may stray away from the intended topic. More time is required than for the lecture.

Discussion can be made more effective by careful preparation. Prepare questions and statements in advance to guide trainees in case they get off track. Watch the time each participant takes and don't let one person monopolize the conversation. Be prepared to redirect the conversation to the intended topic.

## BUZZ GROUPS

Large group discussion is often used to allow for questions and feedback but a far preferable approach is the use of what is termed the buzz group. Buzz groups are subdivisions of a large group—they are small groups of from five to ten people formed for the purpose of discussing a chosen or selected topic. A variation of the buzz group method is the "66" technique, wherein six people are given six minutes to discuss the topic at hand. Some advantages of the buzz groups include the following:

*Involvement of everyone.* Whereas in a large group session or large group discussion only a few voices may be heard, the small group session allows almost everyone to express his or her opinion or thinking on the topic.

*Reduced peer pressure.* People are often hesitant or reluctant to express their opinions in a large group because of fear of what their fellow trainees may think. In a small group session, of course, this pressure is far less apparent and individuals may be much more willing to express their opinions.

*Variety of experience.* The small group session allows for a tremendous variety of experience, knowledge, and background to come to the fore. Whereas in large groups only a few voices are heard, the use of buzz groups in a training session allows a large number of ideas to come forward. This greater volume of ideas, comments, and opinions is of real value to the learning process.

*Exchange of ideas.* Visualize two people seated across the room from one another. One person walks over to the other and hands that person a dollar bill. Before leaving, however, she takes from that person a different dollar bill and then returns to her place. The net result of this, of course, is that each person started with a dollar, and, while it is a *different* dollar, each person also finished with a dollar. Contrast that scene with the exchange of an *idea* rather than a dollar. The net result, of course, is that the person has two ideas instead of the one he or she had initially. This is one of the most important advantages of the discussion technique because it does allow for a free flow of ideas, thus enhancing the totality of all ideas. A far greater volume of ideas can be gathered in a short period of time.

In spite of the many advantages of buzz groups, it must be recognized that there may be some offsetting disadvantages. Some of these include the following:

*Unfamiliarity.* Depending upon the time constraints of the program, it may take some time for the trainee to become acclimated to this technique. For some people, it may be a brand new method and may take some getting used to.

*Voluntary participation.* While it is felt that most people will contribute to the small group discussion, there is no rule that they must do so and some individuals may still feel no desire to participate. While this is a limited drawback, it should be recognized as a possibility.

*Lack of leadership.* Unless the buzz group leaders completely understand their responsibility, the buzz group is nothing more than the proverbial "blind leading the blind." The discussion leader must have been oriented to the situation and should be given some hints as to how to best use the group for participation. Sometimes the buzz group is both leaderless and without direction. The net result is a large waste of time.

*Lack of organization.* Without proper coaching, the individual participant may feel both lost and disorganized. This, of course, hampers the entire training effort.

## ROLE PLAY

The role-play technique allows participants to "play" the role of one or more individuals in a real-life situation. Some of the advantages of role play include:

*Participation.* By definition, the role play directly involves the individuals in the training session. It is usually best to ask volunteers from the group to take part; at times, however, it may be necessary for all members to participate. Rather than select 2 or 3 volunteers, form triads and have each person rotate roles, with the third person acting as an observer who assists in the critique.

*Increased self-confidence.* When the role play involves situations that individuals are likely to encounter, the methods can build self-confidence in a training situation. When the real case occurs, individuals can be more confident knowing they have met and conquered similar situations and are better prepared to deal with such incidents.

*Empathy.* Since the role play involves case studies, individuals have a chance to put themselves in the other person's position. By so doing, they can empathize with both sides of the role.

*Variety of solutions.* Although there may be a "school solution" as such for the role-play method being used, it is far preferable to let the individuals work out the actual solution. Often a variety of possible answers will evolve that can be used in this and future training programs.

*Real world solutions.* The end result of the exercise is typically a practical, usable answer.

Like other methods, the role play is not without its disadvantages as well. Some of the more important items to consider are these:

*Artificiality of situation.* Since the role play is done in an unreal or artificial atmosphere, some participants may have difficulty imagining themselves in the real situation. A classroom or training situation is not the same as a customer's office or other place where the situations being portrayed really will take place.

*Discomfort of participants.* There may be trainees who feel very uncomfortable portraying any type of a role. If the role play involves other trainees acting as observers, some participants may simply go through the motions and the result is far from ideal. If participants are forced to play roles, the play oftentimes overtakes the real work of the program.

*Lack of productivity.* Without proper counseling in advance, the role play is nothing more than a game. If the participants are not convinced that this is a viable and important technique for training, the role play loses all value.

*Time-consuming.* Since this method takes much more time than other types of training, the cost-conscious trainer must be certain that the time is worth the effort. If the role play is given too much time, the participants may lose interest and again all value is lost. Within specified time periods, however, role play performs a function. Role play may be made more effective if the participants are given time to prepare with the help of other group members. They practice before their own group prior to playing before the larger group. Make it a team effort rather than an individual one.

## TASK FORCE

A group can be put together as a task force to find the answer to a specific problem or to research a program to achieve a specified result. In the training situation, the problem or program is structured so that the group must go through an educational process to accomplish its mission.

For example, the group might be required to develop a new, more powerful, replacement part for an electric motor. The first step of the project will require an analysis of the old part. The group will (1) discover that they need to acquire a new knowledge or skill. In the process of analyzing the part, they will (2) prepare themselves by learning the information necessary for the analysis. The task can require a test of the new part. Here the group will (3) gain practice in this new skill. The final research report will provide you with the feedback necessary to determine the success of the learning project, and your grade or comments will in turn provide feedback and will reinforce the behavior of the trainees.

## CASE STUDY

The case study is another important technique that trainers should become familiar with and know how to use properly. The case study is an actual presentation, either written or verbal, of an incident that either did or could happen in a related area. Some schools of business administration rely primarily on the case study as a method of instruction. As with all the other techniques, we should consider both its pros and its cons. Among the advantages of the case study are the following:

*Participation.* After having read or being given the case, small groups typically spend a prescribed period of time discussing it and its possible solutions fully.

*Applicability.* Since the case should be an incident of relevance to the training situation, its "real world" application is obvious. Often the trainee may encounter a similar type of situation after the training program has been concluded.

*Specificity of case.* Since the case should be directly related to the training situation, the training administrator can select or can write those cases that are of real relevance and concern to the group at hand.

Some disadvantages of the case study are as follows:

*Artificiality.* If the case study does not reflect a real-life situation, trainees may view the case as too theatrical and not recognize its applicability to their situation.

*Time consuming.* Depending on the length and scope of the case presented, the time spent in discussion may be far more than is warranted by whatever point is being made. It must be recognized that the case study is a very time-consuming tool.

*Cost.* If commercially prepared cases are not available for or adaptable to particular training situations, the training administrators may be forced to prepare cases themselves. If such is the case, a well-prepared case study becomes very expensive in terms of time and preparation.

*Lack of information.* Too many cases do not give a sufficient number of facts or enough information for the trainees to take action.

*Identifiability.* While the case study should be realistic, if some participants can identify the case as one on which they may have been involved, this will materially stifle their participation. Cases, of course, should be identified as general examples of situations and not identifiable with a specific department or individual in the organization.

## DEMONSTRATION

An excellent way to practice the "show and tell" technique is to use the demonstration to illustrate your points. By simulating actual job situations, the trainer gives the learner a "hands-on" experience. It follows a step-by-step procedure so that every process to be taught can be followed.

Because the demonstration method is best with small groups, there is a cost-benefit factor to consider. For some training situations, it may well be prohibitive on a cost basis. Before discarding it, however, you will want to be certain that its substitute will fulfill your objectives satisfactorily in terms of costs and results.

## NOMINAL GROUP TECHNIQUE (NGT)

A refinement of the small group discussion, the nominal group technique is a method that subtly gets everyone to participate. Designed by Dr. Andre Delbecq at the University of Wisconsin, the NGT approach is an excellent tool that results in high energy and excellent ideas.

The technique suggests these steps for a problem-solving meeting:

• Subdivide the larger group into subsets of 5 to 8 people.

- Pose the open-ended question or problem to the group as a whole.

- Individuals spend a few minutes silently thinking about the questions and jotting down all the responses they can think of.

- Each group lists on a flipchart all the ideas generated. This is done in round-robin fashion and continues until every idea from every person is recorded. This is done without discussion.

- Discussion within each group is now allowed to clarify or expand the items listed on the flipchart.

- Each individual now votes for the top five or top ten (or whatever number is felt to be appropriate). This step can be repeated until the group makes a priority list of 3 to 4 solutions.

- Each subgroup then reports their results to the entire group.

This method can be used in a variety of ways. It is somewhat time-consuming, but the results, both qualitatively and quantitatively, are well worth the investment.

### BUSINESS GAMES

The last few years have seen a surging interest in computer and noncomputer business game exercises. A business game is an activity in which a type of business operation can be "played" over a few minutes or a few hours. It is experientially based and, of course, highly participative.

Sophisticated computer games can run the course of several days, often in concert with other more traditional methods. Once decisions are made, that is, marketing, selling, buying, etc., are fed into the computer, the short- and long-term effects are quickly printed out, thus showing what would likely have happened in real-life situations.

Other types of experiential learning activities or games may be used for a variety of training subjects. These games are often very inexpensive and are excellent for climate-setting. A word of caution, however, is very much in order. Use these games for a specific purpose or to enhance or fortify a skill, knowledge, or attitude. They can be too "gimmicky" or too much fun and, without an expressed purpose, can be counterproductive.

### BRAINSTORMING

A method that merges the discussion technique with a creative twist is a group ideation process called brainstorming. Its purpose is simply to elicit a number of new ideas about and responses to a problem. Unlike a typical discussion or buzz-group method, brainstorming is based on four basic rules:

- Judicial judgment is ruled out.

- "Free-wheeling" is welcomed.

- Quantity is wanted.

- Combination and improvement are sought.

The first rule is the most important. In most business meetings, someone is always ready to throw "cold water" on what we may think of as a "hot idea." Not so in brainstorming. Criticism is not allowed.

In an open, "free-wheeling" system, we are looking for a concept that indicates "the wilder, the better." It may take some training to convince the participants you are, indeed, looking for what some may feel are crazy, outlandish ideas. In fact, as outlined by rule 3, the more, the better. Don't even concern yourself with quality—only quantity.

The last rule prompts us to keep building or "hitchhiking" on previous ideas.

Proponents of brainstorming declare it an excellent way to bring forth new ideas in a creative atmosphere. Critics cite the time-consuming element as wasteful of time and money.

**Figure 6-1.** Rated Effectiveness of Training Methods

| | | | OBJECTIVES | | | |
|---|---|---|---|---|---|---|
| Method | Knowledge | Attitude | Problem-solving Skills | Inter-personal Skills | Participant Acceptance | Knowledge Retention |
| Programmed instruction | 1 | 7 | 6 | 7 | 7 | 1 |
| Case study | 2 | 4 | 1 | 4 | 2 | 2 |
| Discussion | 3 | 3 | 4 | 3 | 1 | 5 |
| Films | 4 | 6 | 7 | 6 | 5 | 7 |
| TV lecture | 5 | 9 | 8 | 9 | 9 | 9 |
| Business games | 6 | 5 | 2 | 5 | 3 | 6 |
| Role play | 7 | 2 | 3 | 2 | 4 | 4 |
| T-Groups | 8 | 1 | 5 | 1 | 6 | 3 |
| Lecture (with questions) | 9 | 8 | 9 | 8 | 8 | 8 |

*Source:* Stephen J. Carroll, Jr., Frank T. Paine, and John J. Ivancevich, "The Relative Effectiveness of Training Methods—Expert Opinion and Research," *Personnel Psychology,* 1972, 25, 495–509.

## A COMPARATIVE LOOK AT METHODS

Several years ago, an article in *Personnel Psychology* entitled "The Relative Effectiveness of Training Methods" discussed the comparative rankings of various methods. Authors Stephen J. Carroll, Jr., Frank T. Paine, and John J. Ivancevich surveyed training personnel and asked them to rank order several methods with specific objectives. Figure 6-1 shows the results.

**Figure 6-2.** Perceived Effectiveness of Nine Training Methods for Six Objectives

| | Knowledge acquisition | | Changing attitudes | | Problem-solving skills | | Inter-personal skills | | Participant acceptance | | Knowledge retention | |
|---|---|---|---|---|---|---|---|---|---|---|---|---|
| METHOD | Mean | Rank | Mean | Rank | Mean | Rank | Mean | Rank | Mean | Rank | Mean | Rank |
| Case study | 3.35 | 4 * | 2.63 | 5 * | 3.89 | 1 * | 2.69 | 5 | 4.40 | 1 * | 3.04 | 4 * |
| Conference (discussion) method | 3.72 | 1 * | 2.93 | 3 * | 2.91 | 5 | 2.89 | 4 | 3.45 | 5 * | 3.26 | 2 * |
| Lecture (with questions) | 2.57 | 8 * | 2.35 | 7 * | 2.47 | 7 | 1.72 | 8 | 2.79 | 8 * | 3.15 | 3 * |
| Business games | 3.27 | 5 | 2.75 | 4 * | 3.68 | 2 * | 2.93 | 3 | 3.57 | 2 * | 2.98 | 7 * |
| Movie films | 2.98 | 6 * | 2.41 | 6 | 2.06 | 9 | 2.00 | 6 | 3.50 | 4 * | 3.00 | 5 * |
| Programmed instruction | 3.49 | 3 * | 2.21 | 8 | 2.85 | 6 | 1.81 | 7 | 2.69 | 9 * | 3.87 | 1 * |
| Role playing | 3.59 | 2 | 3.63 | 2 * | 3.33 | 3 * | 4.06 | 1 * | 3.55 | 3 * | 3.00 | 5 * |
| Sensitivity training (T-group) | 2.74 | 7 | 3.65 | 1 * | 3.00 | 4 * | 3.80 | 2 * | 2.86 | 6 * | 2.57 | 9 * |
| Television lecture | 2.43 | 9 * | 2.20 | 9 | 2.15 | 8 | 1.67 | 9 | 2.81 | 7 * | 2.76 | 8 * |

Rating Scale 5 = highly effective; 4 = quite effective; 3 = moderately effective; 2 = limited effectiveness; 1 = not effective.

*Items with asterisk were deemed acceptable for that objective, as judged in a literature review.

*Source:* John W. Newstrom, "Evaluating the Effectiveness of Training Methods." *The Personnel Administrator,* 1980.

The matrix reveals several interesting questions. For example, you'll note that T-groups (sensitivity training) ranks as number one both for attitude and interpersonal skills. Many experienced HRD professionals may debate that finding. Sensitivity training is not as popular or faddish as it may have once been. Some would even argue that T-group training may have serious and dangerous results insofar as attitude or interpersonal skills are concerned.

Although rated extremely low across the horizontal axis, the lecture (with questions) does have a viable role in the learning process. Properly carried out, the lecture is cost effective and can be an appropriate training method.

In an effort to update this 1972 survey, Dr. John Newstrom, at the University of Minnesota-Duluth, replicated the procedure. His study, conducted in 1979, surveyed training directors from the two hundred largest firms in the United States. With some fifty responses, it does not claim to represent the universe, but it does offer some interesting correlations and comparisons (Figure 6-2).

Note the mean ratings (based on a five-point scale) and relative rankings. Only two items, participant acceptance for the case study method and interpersonal skills for role playing, ranked above the four-point scale. Keep in mind, also, that these are not necessarily the "school solutions." The ratings only record what training professionals from large organizations reported.

## SUMMARY

Let's return to our earlier question. Which method is best? There is no one best method. It depends on the objectives, size of group, time frame, and comfort zone of both trainer and learner.

The preceding list of methods is not intended to be a complete list of methodologies. In fact, there are probably dozens of different methods and techniques available. Our intent was to enumerate some of the more commonly used methods and provide our readers with some pros and cons to consider. Whatever your choice, don't rely only on one!

# CHAPTER 7

# Audiovisuals in Training

*A picture is worth 1,000 words . . .*

### THE VALUE OF AUDIOVISUALS IN TRAINING

This age-old maxim has a definite place in the training process. It is no secret, of course, that people hear and see things differently. We live in a world of visuals; we should also realize that the addition of a visual aid may well contribute to the learning process.

Some studies indicate that of all the five senses, we learn most through sight. As a point of interest, it is estimated that 83 percent of all we learn is learned through sight! On a related note, research indicates that trainees generally remember 10 percent of what they read, 20 percent of what they hear, 30 percent of what they see, and 50 percent of what they hear and see.

Visuals, combined with lectures and other oral presentations, stimulate the auditory and visual senses simultaneously. The crack of rifle fire, for example, backed up by a picture of a hunter holding a smoking gun, leaves no room for doubt about the cause of the noise. To be effective, visuals must support the content of the spoken message. They must relate closely to the narrative and they must be interesting to the participants. If net profit is being discussed, for example, an eye-catching visual can be used to demonstrate graphically the portion of the sales dollar that is profit and the portion that represents the cost of doing business.

The visual portion of the presentation, in keeping with our design policy regarding all elements for evaluation, should be directed toward the achievement of the training goals. Visuals also offer an excellent method for overcoming possible boredom. They provide the variety that keeps the participant attentive.

Some of the main reasons that visuals are so effective are:

*Expectation.* Since the advent of television, people are visual-minded. The influences of home television, movies, and so on have prompted people to simply expect visual aids to be used in meetings.

*Retention.* As indicated earlier, most of what we learn is learned visually. When we rely on only the spoken word to communicate, as much as 75

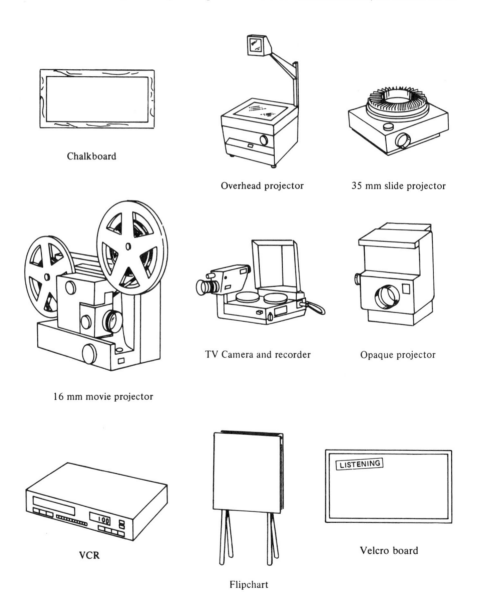

Chalkboard

Overhead projector

35 mm slide projector

16 mm movie projector

TV Camera and recorder

Opaque projector

VCR

Flipchart

Velcro board

percent or more of a message is often misinterpreted or forgotten completely.

*Organization.* Because visual planning prompts the trainer to collect and arrange the lesson content in an orderly fashion, the session is that much better.

## CRITERIA FOR SELECTING AUDIOVISUAL AIDS

In choosing which pieces of equipment to use for your sessions, there is never one best answer. The choices are many and may be determined by such things as:

*Session objectives.* This is perhaps the foremost item for consideration. Just exactly what is the purpose of this session and the desired behavior change? Which acts most closely fit in with your goals? Perhaps a film can best fulfill your objectives in a shorter period of time.

*Group size.* Absurd as it may sound, we occasionally see even experienced trainers attempt to use a flipchart or chalkboard when the size of the group makes those items a poor choice. The statement "I know you can't see this back there, but . . ." is inexcusable! It is the responsibility of the presenter to ensure that the selected visual *can* be seen by all.

While some of these pieces of equipment have an important place in small group meetings, the overhead projector is an excellent replacement for larger groups.

*Size and shape of room.* When training sessions are held in motels, hotels, or other sites away from your own training facility, a host of problems may surface. Most of these rooms were simply not designed with a training purpose in mind, so the preparation and placement of visuals can be very burdensome. Low ceilings, obstructing posts and pillars, too many windows, and so on are but a sampling of problems that must be faced.

*Your preferences.* Like the proverbial old shoe, we may tend to use (and overuse) a particular piece of equipment. While it certainly makes sense for us to become as familiar as we can with visual aids, we must caution ourselves on overreliance on just one item.

There is merit, however, on our becoming expert on one or two particular items. Learn as much as you possibly can about the advantages and disadvantages, and continually quiz other trainers on their experiences. You will gradually amass a wealth of knowledge on those items and will be looked to as a resource in your organization.

*Session content.* Some subjects are simply better geared to a visual approach than are others. The mere fact that already prepared visual material is not readily accessible is not an excuse for bypassing the use of visuals. Even homemade charts, transparencies, chalk-talks, and so on will add life to your presentation. Review your lesson plan and insert visuals where they can best reinforce or emphasize a point.

*Audiovisual assistance.* Most organizations with human resource or training departments will also have some type of audiovisual production resource available. Consult with your colleagues and borrow their ideas liberally. Many large companies and organizations have well-staffed departments that can help you in creating new and exciting visual presentations.

*Costs.* Although most HRD agencies have a multitude of audiovisual aids available, few departments provide a total inventory of everything you may need. With the increasing use of television, many trainers have found it economical to purchase this equipment. Larger cities have audiovisual supply centers and almost all hotels and motels can rent anything you may need in the line of visuals.

*Portability.* If your session is one that will be presented to other personnel at locations across the country, you'll want to check the portability of your chosen items. You may find it less costly to secure items locally rather than transport them with you.

## TYPES OF VISUALS

Let's discuss several of the more commonly used visuals and suggest ways in which they could be used as well as the pros and cons of their use in training situations.

### Chalkboard

Like its predecessor the old-fashioned blackboard, the chalkboard is a commonly used visual. While blackboards are still found in schools and some training facilities, newer adaptations of color and materials are making them obsolete.

Ever wonder why so many of the highway signs are printed in white on a green background? It's the same reason you see so many chalkboards that are green rather than black. It's been proven that this combination (white on green) significantly increases visibility. While a variety of other colors are available, most training rooms and hotels seem to favor the color green.

A newer model, called a whiteboard, offers both visibility and flexibility.

Used with special colored marking pens, these boards are rapidly gaining favor among HRD professionals.

Because whiteboards can also be used as screens for projector use, they provide an added dimension. Many hotels and in-house training facilities have purchased multiuse wall-hanging units that contain a whiteboard, flip-chart, screen, corkboard, and velcroboard. These are excellent for small group training sessions.

Let's look at some of the advantages and disadvantages of the chalkboard:

*Low cost.* Available in a wide variety of sizes, the chalkboard is a relatively inexpensive visual aid. Once purchased, it is a long-lasting tool and needs little maintenance.

*Simplicity.* It takes little experience or preparation to use a chalkboard effectively. Different color chalks or writing materials make its use even more simple and attractive.

*Erasability.* Rather than cluttering up a room with a lot of material that may not be needed later, you can simply erase the chalkboard when its purpose has been served. There are times when one wants to refer back to some material presented earlier but, in most cases, when the point has been completed the material can and should be erased. Another obvious point is that an error or mistake can quickly be removed.

*Flexibility.* It can be used to illustrate most subjects. Portable chalk-boards, available in most hotels, are usually two-sided, thus allowing advance preparation. When the points written on the back are ready to be discussed, merely rotate or flip the surface and continue on.

Like any other visual, the chalkboard is not without its disadvantages. Some of these are:

*Visibility.* For large groups, the chalkboard is not big enough to be effective because it cannot be seen clearly beyond the first few rows of seats.

*Legibility.* Many trainers are not overly proficient in handwriting or drawing skills. A chalkboard bearing information presented in poor or unreadable handwriting is a real disadvantage for the trainee.

*Eye contact.* At times, trainers will make a point while writing on the chalkboard and at the same time talk to the chalkboard. This lack of eye contact precludes complete communication with the audience. Trainers should use the chalkboard to make a few key points and then face the audience for the discussion of these key points.

*Appearance.* Unless previously presented material is neatly and cleanly erased, the chalkboard may appear cluttered or messy. This will distract from an otherwise professional presentation.

**Tricks of the Trade** Experienced trainers have found numerous ways to make the chalkboard an even better medium. Here are some ideas you will find useful.

*Crib notes:* It is a simple task to jot down your crib notes as you use your equipment. For example, with a chalkboard, lightly write in the main points you want to cover. Your audience cannot see your notes and your presentation is greatly enhanced. Don't overuse this technique. This is not the main use of a chalkboard. If this idea appeals to you for continued use, write your crib notes on 3" × 5" index cards and place them in the tray of the chalkboard. They still will not be visible to your audience.

*Colors:* Use different colored chalk or markers to add variety and visibility. When listing points, for example, the use of alternating colors improves note-taking and focuses attention.

*Illustration:* Don't worry if you want to do cartooning, and your artistic skills aren't the best. Make a transparency of the picture or illustration you need and then position the overhead projector using the chalkboard like a screen. If you simply "follow the lines," your illustration will be a perfect reproduction of the original!

*Reference:* Suppose you need to record or save all the items written on the chalkboard for future reference. Borrow a Polaroid camera to take a picture that quickly captures what you need and is handsomely available for review as you need it.

### Overhead Projector

The overhead is perhaps the most versatile of any visual aid. Certainly it seems to be the most often used! A 1983 study published by *Training* magazine indicated that it is used by almost 90 percent of all trainers.

The overhead projector is a machine that is easy to operate and, with minimal practice, it can be used to full effectiveness. With the convenience and accessibility of today's copying machines, transparencies can be made in a moment's time. With blank transparencies or a roller-type attachment, it can be used in lieu of chalkboards or flipcharts.

Some additional advantages are:

*Face-to-face contact.* Everyone can see the screen clearly. The trainer can react to the mood of the audience.

*Note-taking.* You project in full daylight, with no need to darken the room. Hence, note-taking is easy.

*Color.* The addition of colored inks on transparencies adds zest to your projection.

*Good visibility.* By moving the screen or projector, you can enlarge the image, thus assuring good visibility even for large groups.

*Reproduction.* With the use of many copying machines, you can prepare your own visuals. If you want to copy illustrations, a transparency can be projected and traced on a chalkboard or flipchart.

*Focus of attention.* If you are presenting several points and want your audience to focus on each point with you, merely covering the balance of the transparency will direct their attention where you want it.

*Easy reference.* You can always refer back to a transparency. By contrast, work once erased from the chalkboard is lost.

*Reusability.* Individual transparencies or complete sets for projects can be filed away and used over and over again.

*Methodical.* Step-by-step teaching is easy using overlay transparencies. You can reveal material point by point.

Sometimes the disadvantages are reduced by proper utilization of the overhead projector. Sloppily written materials or inadequately prepared visuals do little to enhance the training effort. Also, if transparencies that are too small or too hard to read are used, the overhead is not effective.

### Tricks of the Trade

*Crib notes:* Write your notes on the cardboard frames. Glancing down, you can quickly recall the points you want to make.

*Cartoons:* As indicated with chalkboards, it is a simple task to reproduce any drawing or illustration you need.

*Readability:* Limit your transparencies to a maximum of seven lines. Needless to say, a full typewritten page should not be made into a transparency.

*Colors:* By alternating colors or adding color to your own transparencies, you'll add zest to your session. Incidentally, remember that regular felt-tip pens are not suitable, as they will quickly fade.

*Motion:* Another dramatic attention-getting device can be added through the use of polarized materials that will give an impressive array of color and motion to a transparency. Commercial supply houses sometimes sell these special items. While they can also be produced in house, they are still a novelty to many audiovisual departments.

Many television weather reporters use this same principle when they give their reports. For example, you may have seen such reports where the sun seems to radiate or rain clouds appear to be showering rain. This is often done with polar materials.

*Reverse image:* Newer materials that appear to be opaque are now available in a variety of forms. With a special pen, they chemically remove a film on the sheet and your writing appears. Another variation offers a colored transparency with which a special marking pen can be used to highlight parts of the transparency.

*Attention:* Make sure to turn the machine off when you want the audiences' attention to return to you. If you are using the overhead intermittently with numerous transparencies and prefer not to keep turning the machine on and off, a small piece of cardboard taped to the upper lens of the overhead can be flipped over to block the image. When changing transparencies, always make certain the machine is off to avoid the annoying bright glare on the screen.

*Spotlight:* The overhead can be used as an improvised spotlight for speaker, flipchart, chalkboard, etc.

*Revelation:* By covering up the several items on a transparency, your audience cannot read ahead of the point being discussed. If you use a sheet of paper to do so, place the paper under the transparency so it won't slide off the surface.

*Full-color photos:* You can add a dramatic touch to your presentation by using a full-color photograph. Many office studios can enlarge a colored slide to an 8″ × 10″ transparency. While costly, its impact is impressive.

*Keystone effect:* You can eliminate the distortion of a projected image (keystoning) by shifting either the screen or projector. Many screens now have an extension arm that provides the necessary angle.

### Flipchart

The flipchart is another commonly used aid in training situations. It is inexpensive, easy to use, and can be an attractive addition to the training session. Other advantages include:

*Prepared material.* Professionally prepared material will enhance the training effort. Use of stencils, cartoons, or transfer letters helps make the flipchart a professional and attractive medium. The use of color adds further to the attractiveness of this device. When the flipchart is used in concert with other visuals, the training room becomes a real stage for learning.

*Ease of use.* Since there are no mechanical or moving parts as such, the flipchart is usually a foolproof technique. It requires a minimum of setup time and can be utilized easily.

*Ease of reference.* By using tabs (stapled to the edge of the sheets), the flipchart can easily be returned to earlier points should they be recalled for reference.

*Reusability of material.* Should the content of your session be one that will be repeated frequently, prepared flipcharts are a good choice. If they are prepared neatly and proper care is taken during their use, flipcharts can be used over and over again.

*Accessibility.* If there is any one piece of equipment that seems to be universally found in every training facility, it's likely to be the flipchart. In fact, it has supplemented the chalkboard in many sites. Even in hotel/ motel facilities, flipcharts are becoming increasingly popular when there are no chalkboards mounted to the wall.

*Visibility.* Best used with small groups, the flipchart allows full visibility for group discussion. In demonstrations that require several sheets, the individual sheets are easily removed from the pad and can be taped to any wall surface with masking tape. Posting of these sheets provides full and complete visibility and reference on all items discussed earlier.

*Portability.* With folding easels commonly available, flipcharts are extremely portable. Typically light in weight, these units with a rolled-up flipchart and carrying case can be transported with ease. Table-top and fold-up units are also available.

*Focus of attention.* The same advantage discussed with the use of the overhead is also found in flipcharts. Sheets to be used in a later part of the presentation are, of course, hidden from view until you flip the chart to that particular page. Another variation, using a process of covering points, focuses attention on the respective item you are addressing. By removing the masked portion of the chart, you reveal the items you want to discuss point by point.

**Tricks of the Trade**

*Lining:* If your chart is unlined, simply prepare a lined card that can be placed behind the sheet on which you are working. The card, of course, can be used over and over.

*Bleed:* Because many marking pens tend to "bleed through," use every second sheet. Stapling the two sheets together makes this easier.

*Reverse movement:* Some trainers prefer to use their flipcharts in reverse; that is, instead of the entire pad being flipped over to the back of the easel sheet by sheet, it is far easier to start with the pad entirely behind the easel and merely flip over to the front. Try it and you will find it easier and less noisy.

*Index:* If your presentation is prepared in advance, use small index-type tabs on the side of the sheets. This makes it easy to return to an earlier point. Rather than paging through sheet after sheet until you find the page you want, you quickly locate the tab and easily flip to that spot.

*Cartooning:* If you want to draw cartoons, illustrations, and so on, it is easy to make a transparency in a copying machine and then merely project the transparency on the chart.

*Posting:* If your discussion requires the posting of the flipchart sheets, tape several pieces of masking tape to the back sides of the easel. When you want to post the sheet, your tape is readily available.

*Colors:* If recording a discussion, use alternating colored markers for better visibility. For meetings where minutes are being taken, use the flipchart to write major points or actions taken, then post these for all to see.

*Revelation:* Like the overhead, you can reveal select portions of the chart pad when you want to draw the group's attention to them. By merely folding the sheets to the appropriate place or covering up subsequent points with strips of paper or cardboard, you can uncover the points as you address them.

### 35 mm Slide Projector

The slide or carousel projector can add life to most any training session. Readily available in most facilities, commercial as well as homemade slides can be used. Such a combination can make an attractive training package.

A dramatic presentation can be constructed with the use of two or more projectors, creating a multiscreen result. Other advantages of 35 mm projection are:

*Accessibility.* Every training facility should have at least one such projector available. Even at off-site facilities, these projectors are commonly available from hotel/motel sites or can be rented from commercial audiovisual stores.

*Portability.* The 35 mm projector is easily transported from site to site. Sturdy carrying cases protect the equipment and accessories in transit. In those instances when one prefers not to transport equipment, most carousel-type projectors are compatible and the circular trays are interchangeable. This is not the case, however, with all equipment, so be certain to specify the exact model or brand you need if you choose to rent projectors.

*Professional presentation.* Commercially available sound-slide presentations can be purchased from a number of sources for a variety of training topics and needs. If your organization has a media department or similar agency that provides assistance with audio and visual needs, their assistance can be invaluable in helping you create your own productions. The addition of background music adds polish to your efforts.

*Ease of operation.* The 35 mm projector is relatively easy to operate. Although each model may have different features, each is similar in operation.

*Visibility.* Depending on the size of the screen, the image is adaptable for small and large audiences. Many hotel/motel sites are using white or light-colored wall coverings on at least one part of the room so that the wall can be used when available screens are inadequate for good visibility.

*Flexibility.* For in-house prepared presentations, it is a simple matter to change or revise portions of the slides. For example, in an orientation session showing actual pictures of corporate or organizational VIPs, personnel changes can quickly be taken care of by merely inserting new slides in place of the earlier pictures.

We should also consider a few disadvantages to 35 mm projection. Since a darkened room should be used, it is difficult to take notes. If you are using a room that is hard to darken because of windows or direct sunlight, visibility is greatly reduced. Additionally, some rooms are awkward because of pillars, posts, or their size and shape.

### Tricks of the Trade

*Blank slides:* Always use a blank plastic slide as the first slide and the last slide of a prepared slide presentation to eliminate the glare of the bright screen. Also, with electronic or remote extension cord, the machine can be turned on earlier and you can totally control the presentation without worrying about having someone to turn the machine on or off for you.

*Numbered slides:* Murphy's Law tends to function during slide presentations. Slides often fall out of the carousel at the worst possible time. Number all your slides in the upper right-hand corner; that way, if they should fall out, you will be able to reconstruct the correct order.

*Screen size:* Make certain the projector is positioned far enough away so the image will fill the screen. If that is not possible, elevate the projector so that the image will be at the very top of the screen. Then raise that lower portion of the screen so that the lower part of the projected slide will be at the same level.

*Extra bulbs:* Always carry an extra bulb and know how to replace a burned-out one. Remember Murphy's Law!

*Zoom lens:* The availability of a zoom lens adds a touch of professionalism as well as offering better visibility.

*Computerized slides:* Computer-generated slides are readily available through commercial sources and many in-house audiovisual departments. These are particularly useful for graphs, pie charts, etc.

### 16 mm Projector

Because of the ready availability of hundreds of training films on virtually any topic, the 16 mm projector is another piece of equipment that should be in every training facility. These professionally produced films are available for rent or purchase throughout the country. Other advantages include:

*Ease of operation.* Most recent models of 16 mm projectors are completely self-threading, and if you follow the step-by-step method usually illustrated on each machine, they are simple to operate. Even on older machines, preparation for showing is a simple task. Regardless of the type of machine, you will want to familiarize yourself with the basic workings and mechanics of the projector. Remember, even self-threading machines may occasionally malfunction!

*Authority.* By using films that feature acknowledged and recognized leaders in the field, you can give an air of authenticity to your session. Since many films feature these authorities, it is a relatively inexpensive way to bring the expert to your locale.

*Graphic presentation.* In those cases in which you want to illustrate a skill, films can be used to show closeups and slow motion. By observing mockups in a procedural fashion, trainees can see a methodical progression of the skill being taught. Because of the larger image presented, groups of any size can be trained together.

*Audience involvement.* Some training films are available in which the projector is turned off at various points to allow group discussion on interim points. Certain decision points are incorporated in the film and questions are posed for discussion.

While types that can be turned off at various points are more conducive to audience involvement, *every* film used should be followed by some group discussion. If an instructional guide is not available, as you preview the film in advance of the group showing, develop several questions that you can use after viewing.

You should also be aware of some disadvantages with the use of projectors. Since the room should be darkened, the attention of the group may be hard to maintain. This is particularly true if your session follows a filling meal!

If the film is somewhat dated, the style of fashion (clothing, hair style, and so on) may tend to detract from the film's effectiveness, even though the content may be excellent. Also, if the film has had heavy use, the quality may be less than satisfactory.

**Tricks of the Trade**

*Film clips:* Rather than showing an entire 25–30 minute film, perhaps one or two short 5–10 minute clips of that film may be just as effective. In addition, short "fun" films such as those by the Muppets are available on a variety of meeting planning topics.

*Screen:* Any white or light-colored surface can be used in lieu of a screen. Consider placing the screen in a corner rather than the center of the wall.

*Screen size:* The general rule is that a ratio of six to one be used; that is, for every six feet of distance from the screen, you'll need one foot of screen size. For example, a room 60 feet in length should have at least a 10′ × 10′ full screen; 90 feet means a 15′ × 15′ full screen.

*Malfunctions:* If the film starts "jumping" during the screening, quickly depress the lever near the top sprocket on most machines. If the film keeps jumping after a few such attempts, stop the projector and turn to the "rewind" position. Rewind for just a few seconds and return to the "on" position. That should reframe the film loop to its proper clearance. If that still does not clear the problem, it is necessary to stop the machine and manually readjust the top and bottom film loops.

## Television

The use of television and videotape has rapidly gained popularity and acceptance in human resource development. Frequently used in role play and sales training sessions, it provides immediate feedback for critique and presentation skills.

Some additional advantages are:

*Availability.* Commercial videotapes that cover a multitude of topics can be rented or purchased. Moreover, in-house productions can be easily constructed. Since tapes can be reused, costs are not prohibitive.

*Replay.* For specialized skill-building sessions, the tape can be played over and over again until the skill is mastered. This can be done either on an individual or a group basis.

On the other hand, the equipment may be bulky and not easily transported. Because of the pace of technological change, obsolescence is a factor. Television is best used with smaller groups, but additional monitors could provide added visibility. Costs, too, may be a factor in considering this equipment.

### Tricks of the Trade

*In-house production:* Many training departments regularly produce their own videotapes. The cost is reasonable and the result can be a professional production. Be honest about your skills, however; your audience will expect a first-class production. Anything less is not satisfactory.

*In-house actions:* With proper coaching, company executives and other employees can be used effectively.

*Group viewing:* Since most sets are 23 to 25 inch units, make sure you have a sufficient number of viewing sets available. For some large conferences, the speaker appears on a large screen as well as on several monitors placed throughout the audience.

## Filmstrip

A filmstrip projector with accompanying sound still has a place in the training field. Packaged programs, though limited, are available. An excellent tool for self-instruction and small group demonstration, the filmstrip is an effective visual aid.

However, it is difficult to change or revise the film. This lack of flexibility is the main reason for its limited use.

### Opaque Projector

The opaque projector is similar to the overhead except that it is used to project an image from the original material rather than from a transparency. This page, for example, could be removed from this book, inserted into the opaque projector, and projected onto a screen.

The main advantage of the opaque projector is precisely this ability to project images from original material. It eliminates the cost of preparing transparencies. Drawings or printed matter can be developed on plain paper and instantly projected.

The disadvantages of the opaque projector are its size and bulkiness. Most opaque projectors are rather heavy and cumbersome, and therefore not easily portable. A darkened room is necessary, so note-taking is difficult.

### Flannel Board

As its name implies, a flannel board is constructed with a flocking or flannel material. It can be used to display lightweight cards and items.

It is an effective visual in building a presentation. As each point is discussed, it can be placed on the board. It is very inexpensive and can be constructed using materials bought at any variety store.

### Velcro Board

This device, also known as a hook and loop board, offers complete flexibility for displaying graphics, products, or most any type of training aid. Its principle is simple—namely, rows and rows of hooks and loops that adhere together in a tightly locked fashion (see page 64). Almost any type of object can be displayed. As with the flannel board, one can build points throughout the presentation. It is a dramatic aid in that the viewer is often surprised to see three-dimensional objects displayed so effortlessly.

Its main disadvantage is its bulkiness. While fold-up models are commercially available, they are not easily portable.

### SUMMARY

Visual aids are just that—aids. They should be used to assist the presentation and not as a crutch to replace the presentation. Well-planned visuals can be of real assistance in illustrating or reinforcing your session.

Of the several kinds of visual aids discussed, you will likely choose your own favorites. By becoming completely familiar with a few pieces of equipment, you will soon begin to develop new concepts and ideas to enhance your presentation.

As in any presentation, planning is critical. The room, equipment, outlets, spare parts, and so on must all be checked and double-checked. You will, of course, want to rehearse your session so that you can use the visuals easily and comfortably.

Whether your selection is the simple chalkboard or a multiscreen, multimedia presentation, properly used visuals will make an excellent session just that much better.

# CHAPTER 8

# Computer-Based Instruction (CBI)*

In today's fast-moving world, information has become a precious commodity, and few functions are more important to an organization's success than good, cost-effective training. An effective training program multiplies the value of each employee; helps keep morale up; contributes heavily to better customer service; enables an organization to keep pace with new developments and demands; and impacts profitability.

At the same time, training programs can be difficult to organize, produce, distribute, and evaluate quickly and at a reasonable cost. Piecemeal solutions that require "reinventing the wheel" for each new program waste time and money, and often don't accomplish the training objectives. When that happens, the entire organization suffers.

The increasing importance of employee development and job enhancement have sparked an intensive search for improved instructional tools and methods. Within the last few years, the computer industry has exploded with an array of educational programs and applications. Computers are already playing a role undreamed of a decade ago. Computer-based instruction is proving to be one of the most comprehensive, flexible, and economical instructional systems available to today's trainer.

## WHAT IS COMPUTER-BASED INSTRUCTION?

Computer-based instruction (CBI) and computer-based training (CBT) are several of the generic terms describing the use of computers for learning

---

*   This chapter was written by Jeff King of Westinghouse Electric in Sunnyvale, California. After receiving his masters in education from San Francisco State University, Mr. King spent 14 years with Pacific Southwest Airlines (PSA) in human resource development. As supervisor of computer-based instruction, he was responsible for research, design, implementation, and evaluation of all computer-based instruction.

and training. Computer-assisted instruction (CAI), more specifically, refers to the interaction of a student with a computer for instruction and learning.

The principle behind CAI is not new. The printed programmed learning text, with its blocks of instructional material accompanied by fill-in-the-blank questions and answers, is a rudimentary interactive method of training. The computer takes this technique several steps further by providing instruction tailored to individual needs and abilities. Learning is also bolstered by immediate feedback and positive reinforcement. It is not, however, necessary to take checkbook in hand and buy the latest computer equipment. You do not need a fully computerized system to begin CBI or interactive training to reap its benefits.

## WHY USE COMPUTER-BASED INSTRUCTION?

Before deciding if computer-based instruction is right for your organization, it is critical that you examine your training goals to determine if they will be met by using a computer. In any discussion of the value of CBI there are several points and cost-benefit justifications that are worth considering.

1. Self-paced Instruction Takes Less Time than Group Instruction. When addressing a group, you usually gear toward the lower 25 percent of the group. Thus, instruction is too slow for 75 percent of the students and too fast for approximately 10 percent. Self-paced instruction decreases total training time anywhere from 30 to 50 percent, depending on the study used, and allows students to move at their own pace.

2. Consistency of Information Is Guaranteed. Classroom instruction permits variation of delivery and content between instructors, depending upon style and level of technical knowledge. CBI programs contain the most accurate information possible. They also offer the program to each individual in exactly the same format and text, thereby ensuring that each student gets the same information.

3. Simulations Free Up Expensive Equipment and Inventory. Most systems available offer the capability to simulate equipment and other computer systems. This permits the productive use of the equipment and inventory instead of dedicating it to training. For example, if CBI is being used to instruct on the use of a keypunch machine, a simulation of the keyboard and pertinent operations is created in the training system and practice can then be given while the keypunch is still in operation. Simulations can be done on computer, videotape, or videodisk. In many cases, this cost benefit can offer an ROI (return on investment) for the purchase of the CBI system within the first year based on the savings from equipment costs related to training.

4. Travel and Related Costs Can Be Cut. If centralized training is used for many remote locations, travel can be the most costly part of training. The related costs include hotel, meals, and, in many cases, overtime expenses or temporary replacement for longer classes over and above training costs.

5. Training Is Available Where and When It Is Needed. CBI eliminates the logistical problems associated with training. People can be trained when you need them trained, not just when the training is scheduled. You can also decrease the problem of new hires being unproductive while waiting for a class to be scheduled. As a job support vehicle, CBI offers review and updating/upgrading of personnel during nonpeak times and at the job site.

When estimating the cost benefits, always take into consideration the unique requirements of the organization and the capabilities of the system you choose.

## DETERMINING YOUR NEEDS

Before beginning the search for the best system available for CBI, determine what you want to use CBI for and what capabilities the system must have to accommodate your training needs and goals. The array of options and capabilities is almost endless. Start by asking yourself the following questions:

- How many people will use the system at any one time?

- Are there programs available on the open market that are applicable to our needs? If so, which operating system are they written for?

- Do I need the capability to create my own programs—called "authoring"—or would I be able to customize existing prepackaged programs?

- Do I want the capability for graphics? Color? Animation?

- How important is a student record-keeping system?

- Is it important that the system be stand-alone or can it be a part of a network using the phone lines and a modem to operate?

Each of these questions poses a unique problem. Finding one system that contains all of the parameters you set will be a real challenge.

There are many personal computers (PCs) that can run the assortment of training programs offered by a variety of companies. Investigate these programs before deciding on a system; often they are more cost effective than a "create your own" system. They have their limitations, however, so research all of the options before committing yourself. Find out if the programs you are building a training program around and buying hardware to run really *are available* and *do* meet your training needs. If they require a data processor to input the courses, be sure to find out if one is available and the estimated cost of acquiring the knowledge of the system. On the other hand, if you've decided on the need for the authoring capability, be sure to request a demonstration of the software. Many times you will find that a computer salesperson will have a definition of "user friendly" that may not be the same as yours.

## DESIGNING AN INTERACTIVE COMPUTER-BASED PROGRAM

Before you begin to design a computer-assisted instruction program, it is important to remember why you want to use the interactive format. It is easy to fall prey to technology and assume that CAI is the answer to all training questions. Prior to deciding on the design format, identify the objectives of the program. How will interactivity enhance those goals? Some subject matter does not lend itself to the interactive format. This includes technical training and the completion of forms. If, however, a computer or similar piece of equipment that is based on an interactive approach is used in the actual job, then CAI could be an effective approach.

When beginning to design your program, remember that flexibility is one of the keys to success in CAI. The program must anticipate the needs of the student and have the necessary information available in the program. You must provide material that will appeal and inform at many different competency levels.

For example, when approaching a management development training program on interviewing skills, you might assume that the approach to use is to begin with the basic skills and continue with a case study to test competency. In a CAI program, the student should be allowed to go directly to the case study if they demonstrate awareness of the basic skills. The case study should cover all of the topics in the basic program and test to ensure understanding of the key principles. In other words, you don't force all students to go through the entire course, but you do design the case study so that no one can complete it correctly without an understanding of the basic skills.

Overcoming the hesitancy of many first-time users is a major challenge to the design of a successful CAI program. This is why many professionals build in either a HELP key or begin each of their programs with a question about how to use the system. Based on the response to that question, designers might "branch" the student to the lesson or out to another lesson that demonstrates how to use the system. The term *branching* refers to the practice of bringing the student to different parts of the program based on their responses to questions answered. Without an understanding of the commands and the language of the system in use, the student will find it impossible to correct a mistake or begin again. This is especially important because a major problem facing many students is a fear of the machine; if the system acts up, they may literally unplug the equipment and walk away.

There are many different formats and instructional design models available for CAI programs. One of the simplest of these models is the linear approach (see Figure 8–1).

In this approach, the student starts on the left side of the scale and, through a combination of information and test questions, moves toward the goals of the program on the right. The information ranges from the basic to intermediate level, and finally to the more advanced level. The methodology is to give information, immediately test for competency, and then to move to the next level. The major drawback to this approach is the lack of reinforcement and selective retraining based on specific problems.

The next approach outlines the branching of the program to better meet the needs of the students. In the program flow chart (Figure 8-2), the branches are based on the responses to the self-tests and to specific questions about the use of the program. The final exam tests comprehensive knowledge, while the self-tests identify specific core material information.

In the flow chart in Figure 8-2, students enter the system and are immediately asked if they know how to use the system. Based on the answer, they either go to the actual program or to an external program that teaches them how to use the system. Once they have completed the external program, they are brought back to the original lesson they requested. After presentation of the material, they are given a self-test. If the answer is incorrect, they are branched back to the original program to reinforce their learning. They can then try again after rereading the material. If the students answer correctly, they move on to the next question (self-test question #2). The branch here is either to new material or to a third question. If they answer the third question correctly, they can continue in the program. If the answer is incorrect, they are branched to another external program, which breaks down the information presented in the original module and

**Figure 8–1.** Linear Design Model

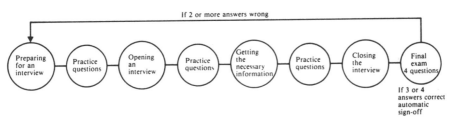

**Figure 8–2.** Program Flow Chart

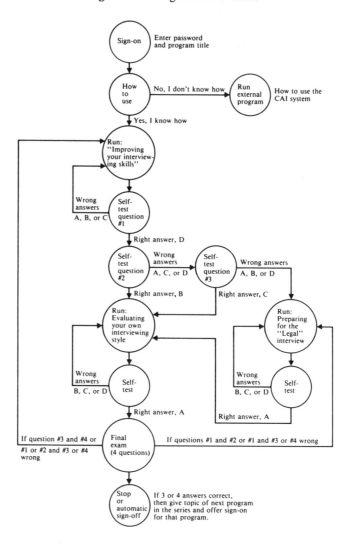

presents a different approach. Once they have read the program and answered the questions correctly, they are branched back to the original lesson. The culmination of the program is a final exam, which covers the material in the complete course. Based on the percentage of correct answers, they can either be signed off or branched to the beginning of the lesson to review all of the information covered.

This model can be expanded by the use of menu selections. The menu contains all of the subject matter covered in the lesson and allows the student to target specific problem areas for review or training and go directly to them.

## SUMMARY

In this chapter we have looked at computer-based instruction and identified some of the uses and benefits to an organization. The interactive approach can be incorporated into your existing training programs and, as your organization develops, the introduction of CBI can enhance your training efforts.

When choosing a computer system to design and deliver your training programs, bear in mind that the first priority is to identify what is necessary and what is desired. Start with a small approach and work toward a full-blown CBI network.

Flexibility is the key to CBI. As your students become familiar with the CBI format, you will need to alter and adjust to ensure that they do not become so aware of the design and format that they lose the real intent of the lesson.

# CHAPTER 9

# Communication

*You cannot not communicate!*

While this statement may not be grammatically correct, it is *totally* correct in the real world of human resource development. Think about it. Anytime you're around people, it's all but impossible not to communicate. You may not even utter a word, but people "read" you all the time. And as we're sure you'll agree, the unspoken word sometimes may "speak" more loudly than anything else. So whether you're leading a group training session or are in a group practicing quiet meditation, it's a sure bet that you're communicating.

Ask a dozen trainers to define *communication* and you'll likely get a dozen different answers. Probably few words are used so often with so little common understanding. This chapter will first suggest a definition for *communication,* then identify some goals for our communication efforts, and, finally, build a chain of communication. Since communication presents a possible problem area for many of us, we will enumerate several barriers to effective communication and offer some techniques for helping us to improve our training efforts by improving our communication ability.

## DEFINITION

The dictionary and other sources list several different meanings for *communication.* Consider these:

> The art or fact of imparting or transmitting . . . facts or information communicated . . . a letter, note, or other instance of written information . . . interchange of thoughts or opinions: a process by which meanings are exchanged between individuals through a common system of symbols (as language, signs, or gestures) . . . an art that deals with expressing and exchanging ideas effectively in speech or writing. . . .

For our purpose, let's use the following as a basic yet workable definition: "Communication is the mutual exchange of information and understanding by any effective means."

What we are saying is that to be effective, communication must have mutuality of understanding. Unless we have a two-way street, there simply is no communication. Giving information is not enough; just because a person hears does not necessarily mean that person also understands. Take, as an illustration, a trainer dutifully reading from a lesson plan to a room full of trainees. Is this communication? Of course not, but how often do we find ourselves doing about the same thing? One-way communication is *not* communication!

Our definition ended with the words "by any effective means." In other words, it includes body language or kinesics. As you fully realize, communication can be spoken, written, heard, or seen. While much of our time as trainers is spent communicating verbally, we often "communicate" by not saying a word! In fact, often our body language will "speak" much more loudly or emphatically than will the spoken or written word. Kinesics, unconsciously transmitted to an astute observer, will either reinforce or contradict our verbal utterances.

For example, an instructor pounding on the podium may communicate very clearly. By the same token, a new employee who nervously fingers his collar while sitting in on your training program also communicates.

In brief, we, as trainers, are always communicating.

## IMPORTANCE OF COMMUNICATION IN TRAINING

We've all seen teachers who can't teach and perhaps even trainers who can't train. We could be the world's foremost authority on any given topic, but if we had difficulty transmitting and transferring that knowledge to others, we would be totally ineffective in our training.

Why is so much importance placed on communication in today's organizational setting? For one reason, it's the number one problem in most firms, agencies, and organizations. As a trainer, you will be able to sell your ideas if you can communicate effectively. Whether you are in business, industry, government, education, or a service organization, the ability to express yourself clearly can be your most valuable asset.

Regardless of anyone's job, the most important part of that job is dealing with people. As John D. Rockefeller once stated, "The ability to deal with people is as purchasable as sugar or coffee and I will pay more for that ability than any other under the sun."

Communication is becoming an increasingly popular term in all phases of human resource development. Hardly a day passes that some slip-up, some problem, or some error is not laid to a "breakdown in communication." It becomes a handy scapegoat.

Experts tell us that as much as 70 percent of our communications efforts are likely to be misunderstood, misinterpreted, rejected, disliked, or distorted; in other words, we operate at only a 30-percent efficiency rate. While a .300 batting average is fine for baseball, the game of training demands a much better mark!

To further pinpoint the importance of communication, you need only ask yourself the question, "How much time do I spend in communicating?" If today for you can be considered an average day, what percentage of your time did you spend in some form or phase of communication, for example, reading, writing, listening, or speaking?

That question has been researched time and time again, and the results are uniformly shocking. The average person spends 80 percent of his or her waking hours in some form of communication! Now begin to compare that with your own percentage. Increasingly, and perhaps surprisingly, we find most trainers well above that 80 percent rate!

Now we have an obvious question for you: How much are you paid to communicate? Now then, in comparing and contrasting that earlier mentioned 30-percent efficiency factor with your own efficiency rate, would you say you are overpaid or underpaid?

## GOALS OF TRAINING COMMUNICATION

We spoke earlier of keeping behavioral objectives in mind while preparing lesson plans and training sessions. So, too, for our communication efforts we should have some specific goals in mind. Here are a few for consideration:

*To change behavior.* It would seem evident that our first goal would coincide with what learning is all about—effecting a change in the behavior of our participants. Through effective training and effective communication, we can alter patterns of behavior.

*To get action.* You've all heard management defined as "the art of getting things done through others." Let's amend that just a bit to "the art of getting the *right* things done through others." Isn't it strange that there never seems to be enough time to do things right the first time, and yet there's *always* time to do them over!

Through effective training your participants will learn how to get the job done. Work simplification experts tell us that there is always a better way. Effective communication helps your participants learn a better way.

*To give (get) information.* New subject matter, skills, or attitudes are conveyed through training sessions. Remember, it's not only the "what" of a topic, it's also the "why."

*To ensure understanding.* Closely aligned to the preceding goal, this involves giving as well as receiving understanding. Through the two-way communication effort, your instructional technique helps ensure that your participants really understand the content being presented. Coupled with this problem of understanding, we must be ever alert to prevent misunderstanding!

*To persuade.* Setting a climate for the self-motivation of your participants is an important task. Persuasive communications can assist in this effort. After all, you are selling your ideas and concepts to your participants.

## A COMMUNICATION CHAIN

Think for a moment of a recent training session, conference, or meeting when things didn't seem to go quite right. In retrospect, can you pinpoint the reason for an unsatisfactory result? In this section, we will construct a chain of communication and identify the links in this chain. Effective communication demands a strong chain with equally strong links. Your total effort will be only as strong as the individual elements that comprise it. Here are the links:

*Sender.* You as the trainer, or sender, of the communication are totally responsible for the chain's sturdiness. Unless you have a clear and complete understanding of the message, content, or concept you are presenting, it is extremely presumptive to assume your participants will really learn. As you begin to prepare your material for presentation, study these questions:

- Who?—Who am I speaking to? What kind of people are they? Do they know enough about this subject to act on my message? Who should be told?

- What?—What is the purpose of this message? What am I trying to say? What background information should I pass on? What things should I leave out? What is the best medium to use?

- Why?—Why is it important? Why should they receive the information? Why is this change being made?

- When?—When should I tell them? When will they be ready for this?

- How?—How should this be communicated? How can I be sure they will learn?

*Idea.* Unless you have a clear idea of the message and its purpose, there is little likelihood you can communicate it effectively. One of the most common causes of communication breakdown is that the sender doesn't understand the message. The sender must be able to express the idea in words, symbols, or sounds that can be easily understood.

*Information.* In your sessions, you should provide a sufficient amount of factual information for the learner. Unless there are enough facts for proper action, the participant is left wanting and the chain breaks down.

*Language.* Occasionally in oral and written communication, trainers use "25- and 50-cent words" that are really meant to *impress* rather than *express*. These words may look very nice on paper or sound quite eloquent when heard, but if they are not understood, they are not performing their task. Your job is to inform, not necessarily to impress. You needn't be ashamed of choosing a short, commonly used word in place of a five-syllable "tongue twister" that no one can understand.

*Medium.* Your method of instruction or visual aid is always an important consideration. The lecture method is perhaps appropriate for large groups, but coupled with another method (TV or discussion, for example) it becomes a more effective device.

Computer-assisted instruction is another medium becoming more popular in human resource development. Whatever your choice, select media carefully to strengthen your presentation. Remember too that audiovisual aids are just that—*aids*—and used strategically will strengthen your chain.

*Receiver.* The receiver, of course, is the learner. In group learning activities, it is difficult to ascertain whether each person completely and fully understands the session content. By learning more about their background, experience, age, and job descriptions, you can tailor the content to the wants and needs of your participants.

As shown here, the chain is a closed system. The sender and receiver must obviously be in tune with each other. Unless we are on the same

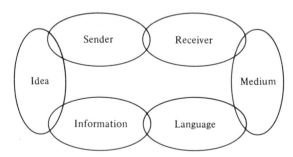

wavelength, there is no communication. Damage one link and the chain weakens.

Return now to an earlier question—think of a recent session that never reached its mark. Now review the six links in our chain and analyze which one(s) were the culprit. Most often, the very first link—the sender—is the weak link in the chain.

## BARRIERS TO EFFECTIVE COMMUNICATION

Why is it that things do go wrong so often in communication? Why is it that our participants can't or won't understand?

There is not a reader who, at this very moment, can't think of two or three recent incidents that would illustrate such problems.

What are the barriers that block clear understanding? Let's look at a few common ones that typically affect the training session.

*Perception.* If you were asked to describe the picture you see below, what would your answer be? Would you spend some time telling us the virtues of the young lady pictured and go on in great detail about the fine person she is? Or would you tell us instead about the wonderful *old* lady and describe her characteristics?

Yes, there are two pictures here. If you see only one, you may have some difficulty seeing the other. If you saw the picture of the young lady first, you must change your perspective to see the old lady. In studying the picture, keep the dark hair and heavy coat as they were. Looking then at

the young lady's chin, you will slowly see it transform into the old lady's nose; her left ear becomes the old woman's left eye; the young woman's neckband soon appears as the older person's mouth. And so on until the image is complete.

In short, if we "get the picture" of the old lady while the person to whom we are talking sees the young lady, there really is no communication. As is now evident to you, the picture contains both a young and an old lady. Do you get the picture?

There is an interesting point here. If you saw only one picture at first, you might admit to having a rather difficult time finding the other. How often has it happened that once we get our mind set, or once we see things our way, we have difficulty empathizing with someone else? The adage "My mind is already made up, don't confuse me with the facts," is all too appropriate. This barrier is perhaps the single most important one in all of communication. People see things differently. Your participants will often "see" what they want to see. Your efforts will help them "see" what the session purports to teach.

*Language.* We've already touched briefly on the language problem. Trainers often fall prey to this trap. As we said, communication is for expression— not impressing. Here is a classic story that serves to illustrate. It concerns an exchange of letters between a plumber and an official with the National Bureau of Standards.

Bureau of Standards
Washington, D.C.

Gentlemen:

I have been in the plumbing business for over 11 years and have found that hydrochloric acid works real fine for cleaning drains. Could you tell me if it's harmless.

Sincerely,

Tom Brown, Plumber

Mr. Tom Brown, Plumber
Yourtown, U.S.A.

Dear Mr. Brown

The efficacy of hydrochloric acid is indisputable, but the chlorine residue is incompatible with metallic permanence!

Sincerely,

Bureau of Standards

Bureau of Standards
Washington, D.C.

Gentlemen:

I have your letter of last week and am mightily glad you agree with me on the use of hydrochloric acid.

Sincerely,

Tom Brown, Plumber

Mr. Tom Brown, Plumber
Yourtown, U.S.A.

Dear Mr. Brown:

We wish to inform you we have your letter of last week and advise that we cannot assume responsibility for the production of toxic and noxious residues with hydrochloric acid and further suggest you use an alternate procedure.

Sincerely,

Bureau of Standards

Bureau of Standards
Washington, D.C.

Gentlemen:

I have your most recent letter and am happy to find that you still agree with me.

Sincerely,

Tom Brown, Plumber

Mr. Tom Brown, Plumber
Yourtown, U.S.A.

Dear Mr. Brown:

Don't use hydrochloric acid. It eats hell out of the pipes!

Sincerely,

Bureau of Standards

We are certain that Tom finally got the message! And that's what communication is really all about.

*Semantics.* Closely connected is the meaning of words themselves. One must quickly accept the fact that the multiple meanings of words present a serious roadblock to communication. Of the thousands of words in the English language, the five hundred most frequently used words have an average of some twenty-eight different meanings! Think of the confusion inherent in that alone.

To illustrate, the word *round* has over seventy meanings. The word *fast* also has many meanings, some of which are contradictory. For example, a "fast" color is one that won't run; a "fast" horse runs very well. Watch this when you are preparing lesson plans.

*Inflections.* It's not what you say, it's how you say it. Tomorrow, experiment with a simple "Good morning" to your staff and watch the reactions. A cheery salutation communicates to all that a good day is in store; a grumpy "G'morning" conveys the opposite.

Repeat this statement aloud with emphasis on the italicized words and watch the different meanings result.

"*I* didn't say he was a lousy trainer."

The meaning here is one of a disclaimer.

"I *didn't* say he was a lousy trainer."

Here, a direct denial.

"I didn't *say* he was a lousy trainer."

Although not put in words, the implication is still clear.

"I didn't say *he* was a lousy trainer."

You see, it still *is* a lousy trainer.

And so on. Your participants may read between the lines, so be aware of these obstacles.

*Personal interests.* When the subject matter personally affects the trainee, communication efficiency picks up considerably. Instead of always talking of my interests, let's instead speak of you and your interests. Too many of us forget that the most important word in the English language is *you.* When we talk in terms of the other person, that person becomes involved and a more effective communication results.

*Emotions.* As we all know, emotions often produce devastating obstacles to good communications. In any person-to-person relationship, emotions play a prominent role. If they are kept in check, no problems arise. But let one person say the wrong thing—and blast off!

If we recognize that emotions can play havoc in dealing with others, this barrier can be minimized. Sensitive topics or words (called red-flag words) must be identified and treated with care.

Incidentally, it's important to remember that emotions play a part in *every* communications attempt. What a person means may not really be what that person says, and often what the heart hears is quite different from what the ear hears. For example, "Good job, Mr. Smith," may really be interpreted by Smith as ("Nice job, my foot, what's he trying to get out of us this time?").

*Preconceived notions.* All too often, we make assumptions and later wish we hadn't. In communications, we may see something and make inferences that are not valid. Looking at this illustration, try reading the message:

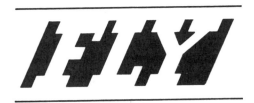

If you can't see the word *FLY*, don't worry. It's there, but experience shows that only about one in four will see the word. (If you're still having trouble, concentrate on the white space instead of the black markings.) The point is simple. In the figure, a first glance may have communicated several computerized symbols (the only meaning we could infer, perhaps, from the seemingly unintelligible signs).

But how many times have wrong actions been taken because of "I thought you meant . . . !"

*Attention.* Essential to getting one's message through to another person is the attention of the receiver. In training programs, we must keep the session interesting and informative enough to both capture and maintain the interest of the participants. We've all been in situations where we've been subjected to an overly long and boring presentation. While we were undoubtedly physically present, mentally we may have been miles away!

*Wordiness.* Becoming too wordy in both verbal and written communications invites the receiver to turn off the sender. We've all heard the speaker who goes on and on or who beats around the bush without ever making a point. As we politely sit through such a session, we wonder just what it is the speaker is driving at.

In writing lesson plans, don't say in a paragraph what can be written in one sentence. Time is far too precious to be wasted in words or pages that don't contribute to the input of the message.

*Inferences.* Many of us jump to conclusions before all the facts are in. We often make assumptions or inferences that later may prove to be incorrect. "But I thought you said," "But didn't you mean," and statements like these often follow a communication where inferential thinking may have led us astray.

We see or hear or read something and may think it means something quite different from what the sender intended it to mean.

Try this exercise: Quickly read aloud the phrases in these three triangles:

Try it again. It may take a few attempts before you detect the use of double articles in each phrase.

But don't worry—most of us don't catch the correct statement initially. "But I thought it said . . ." is a common response. In training, or in any communication effort, watch the assumptions barrier.

### LISTENING

How well do you listen?

Some years ago, Loyola University in Chicago conducted an interesting survey. For eighteen months, researchers attacked this single problem: "What is the single most important attribute of an effective manager?" Based on interviews with thousands of workers, the result was summarized thusly: "Of all the sources of information a manager has by which he can come to know and accurately size up the personalities of the people in his department, listening to the individual employee is the most important."

A basic reason why most of us are poor at listening is that we practice it so seldom. Though few of us have been taught how to listen, listening efficiency can actually be raised by merely giving some attention to it.

A prime cause of poor listening is the difference between the "think" speed and a person's rate of speech. This refers to the difference between the average rate of speech—about 125 to 175 words a minute—and the brain's capacity to "think" words, which is at the rate of 500 to 1,000 words a minute or, in some cases, 5,000. An analogy is a person traveling 55 miles an hour in a car and seeing a jet overhead traveling at 550 miles an hour. Clearly, the car is left hopelessly behind. So, too, with listening. The brain works so fast that the relatively slow input of those 125 to 175 words a minute leaves the mind much room to meander mentally about other things. You can prove this point next time you are engaged in conversation. At times, the listener will be "miles away." Your participants will tune you in and tune you out dozens of times, even in a brief presentation.

### Improving Your Listening

Your role as a trainer includes a responsibility to speak effectively and to listen actively. By listening carefully to your participants, you can gauge how your session is being received. By listening patiently to their comments and questions, you can tell how well your points are being understood. Your participants can use the following ideas to improve their basic listening in the training session. And you can put them to use to improve your overall listening ability.

*Give feedback.* When you are giving or being given instructions, immediate feedback is very important. "So what you're saying, Miss Jones, is . . ." clarifies the meaning on the spot. If there is a misunderstanding, the best time to rectify it is immediately to avoid future problems.

*Listen between the lines.* Very often, we may say one thing while we really mean something quite different. Your participants may do this also. So it is important to remember this advice: "Don't listen to what I *say,* listen to what I *mean!*"

*Listen for ideas.* Every speaker hopefully has a purpose, but it may not relate to the content of the speech. In order to determine the speaker's motive, free your mind of traditional evaluative thoughts and ask yourself the question: What is the speaker's purpose? Listen carefully and get an idea of the speaker's perspective. Try to understand the framework and point of view.

By listening carefully, without overdue emphasis on evaluating, you learn new details, gain new ideas, develop new insight, and may even create an obligation for the other person to listen to you!

*Listen for attitudes.* Our behavior is a reflection of our attitudes, and our attitudes are shaped by our motives. To understand a person's motives, you must listen carefully for expressions about other people, classes, groups, or ideas. People reveal their attitudes in their comments about others. Research has shown that people attribute their own attitudes to other people or groups, except when they clearly distinguish between themselves and the group they are discussing. So listen attentively and don't let a contrasting attitude or value stop you from listening.

*Avoid negative feedback.* To determine people's motives, you must provide an open setting. The environment must be one in which the speaker feels free to express opinions, feelings, ideas, and attitudes, without recrimination. These expressions, attitudes, and so on are all clues to motives and must be encouraged.

Two generally unrecognized forms of negative feedback that block free expression are (1) emotional reactions and (2) negative nonverbal reactions. When people become emotionally upset they tend to interrupt, argue with, or criticize the speaker. This, of course, is not listening and it immediately throws the speaker on the defensive.

If you feel disturbed or angry with a trainee's comments, remember that you will be better able to deal with the situation if you fully understand the opposing position. Count to ten, imagine yourself blowing your top, or think of the irony—the comic side—of listening empathetically to something that disturbs you. If you are to learn others' motives, you must keep your cool and avoid emotional reactions.

Negative nonverbal feedback must also be avoided. Think what would happen if in the middle of a participant's presentation you started shaking your head, indicating the student was wrong. This negative feedback could completely destroy the student's confidence and cause suppression of further ideas and opinions. Although no one would consciously do such a thing, many people unconsciously send the same message through less obvious nonverbal behaviors. A bored manner, or a look of disparagement, question, or surprise could have the same effect. Any of these nonverbal behaviors or a stern gaze might create discomfort on the part of the speaker.

The best way to avoid negative feedback is to provide positive feedback. If you smile, give your group undivided attention, and occasionally nod your head in approval, you are already giving positive reinforcement.

*Empathize.* Perhaps the best trait of a good listener is that of empathy. Being able to put ourselves in others' places and sincerely trying to see things from their point of view is truly an ability trainers should cultivate.

Listening is an active art that can be improved. Empathetic listening is an elusive art that can be learned. For example, "I can see why you feel that way" immediately tells the other person you're trying to be fair. Practice empathy and watch your listening efficiency rise.

## WRITTEN COMMUNICATION

Although a comprehensive treatise on written communication is beyond the scope of this book, it is pertinent to touch on the topic as it relates to lesson planning.

Certainly all of the principles, goals, and barriers discussed earlier apply to our written efforts as well.

The task of writing is often an arduous one for many trainers. It must be acknowledged that putting ideas, concepts, or activities on paper can be very difficult. What might seem simple or commonplace to *do* is often very difficult to *say* or to *write*. To prove that, let's suppose your task right now is to write a lesson plan to teach someone how to tie a shoe. Sound simple? OK, here's some space to write out your instructions.

_____

_____

_____

_____

_____

_____

Give up? You can now sense the problem of written communication.

When you write your lesson plans, give them a trial run with family, friends, or colleagues. Let your audience assist you by pointing out ambiguities, unclear terms, or other barriers we mentioned earlier.

## SUMMARY

Effective communication is the very heart of all human resource development. The transmittal of knowledge, attitudes, and skills is really what training is all about.

All of us spend a majority of our time trying to communicate. All too often our efforts may fall short because our goals were not clarified or known by us or the receiver. We can improve our ability to communicate by remembering to synthesize all the links of the communication chain into a meaningful message. By overcoming roadblocks and obstacles that may preclude effective communication, we can also enhance our efforts.

Listening is an active art, not a passive science.

We can also better our own listening efforts by tuning in to the underlying statements of our participants. With true empathy, we're well on the way.

# CHAPTER 10

# Principles of
# Learning

*OK, here I am—learn me 'sumthin'!*

Hopefully, you will never hear a trainee communicate that verbally, but you may "see" a trainee communicate it nonverbally!

Our purpose in this chapter is to look at the field of adult learning in a very basic way and present to you—in a practical manner—theory and research findings about the way we learn. Some trainers are afraid to discuss the principles of learning because they hesitate to get involved in the maze of educational theories. You will soon see why these fears are unfounded because much of what we know about the way we learn is based on common sense and thoughtful application. Let's start.

## SOME DEFINITIONS

Before we get too involved with principles and learning, let's begin with some understanding of these two terms. A quick check of the dictionary shows:

Principle: a general truth or law, basic to other truths; a comprehensive or fundamental law, doctrine, or assumption.

Learning: knowledge obtained by study; the act of acquiring knowledge or skill; a mental activity by means of which skills, habits, ideas, attitudes, and ideals are acquired, retained, and utilized, resulting in the progressive adaptation and modification of behavior.

Learning is a lifelong process in which experience leads to changes within the individual. It has also been defined as self-development through self-activity. Learning is a change in behavior resulting from experience. In brief, learning means change!

## CHANGE

For many people, this change in behavior causes concern. As a matter of fact, for many trainees (and trainers!), any change is uncomfortable. It is a well-known fact that people tend to resist change. A less well-known fact is that people don't resist change as much as they resist *being* changed. At any rate, change may be uncomfortable for many of us. Perhaps we can prove this to you with a simple exercise:

Fold your arms as you normally would in front of you. Without glancing down, can you tell which arm is on top? Quickly now, unfold your arms and refold them the opposite way. For many of us, this presents no problem. For some, however, it is an awkward, uncomfortable activity.

You might also try this one:

Clasp your hands together so that thumbs and fingers are interlaced. Glance down and note how they are placed together. Then undo them and quickly reclasp your hands in exactly the opposite way. Again, for some of us, our thumbs and fingers got in the way! Change can be difficult! These two activities may help you better empathize with your trainees as they encounter new experiences and new learning activities.

## PEDAGOGY, ANDRAGOGY, AND SYNERGOGY

*Pedagogy,* the term generally used to describe the art and science of teaching children, comes from a Greek derivation, *paid* meaning "child" and *agogus* meaning "leader of." As still practiced in most levels of formal education (and malpracticed in college and training environments), it is largely a teacher-centered approach to learning. Ostensibly, it was the teacher's role to teach and the learner's role to learn—albeit, a passive and dependent one.

*Andragogy* refers to the art and science of helping adults to learn. This term was coined by Dr. Malcolm Knowles, a noted lecturer and author in the field of adult education. Its underlying foundation is simply that adults learn differently from children and that, in applying learning techniques to the field of human resource development, we should realize that our trainees are not kids and should not be treated as such.

Unfortunately, many of our college and university faculty members tend to overlook that basic fact of life! We've all seen teachers who can't teach and we've also observed trainers who can't train. Perhaps if more of our colleagues would acknowledge the premises of Dr. Knowles's theory, we could all witness an upgrading in both the teaching and the learning business. The andragogical theory of learning makes these assumptions about adults:

*The need to know.* Once we are sold on *why* learning the new skill, knowledge, or attitude is important, the motivation to learn follows. Without this knowledge, resistance could result. The more adults can understand the importance of the "need to know," the more effective and positive will be the learning experience.

*The need to be self-directing.* Most participants in our HRD programs want to be self-respecting, responsible for their actions and activities, and involved in directing them. We have a strong need to take responsibility for our own lives. If possible, we want to have a hand in designing our learning activities. This self-directed learning, however, does not necessarily mean learning without help. Self-directed adult learners use networking and secure assistance whenever needed. Because participants come to our programs with this experience, they are a keen resource for the astute trainer. Correctly used, these areas of background and expertise can enrich the training effort.

*Experience.* Adults have more experience. Simple and obvious as this statement is, too many of our training and development friends seem to ignore it. Adults can help each other learn. In fact, this type of supportive learning can be very effective. If we can ferret out this experience and make it an integral part of the learning process, then we indeed are learning from each other.

*Readiness to learn.* Adults must be ready to learn. This means that our participants must be ready, able, and willing to learn before we can ever hope to teach them. Unless there is an innate motivation and an acknowledged readiness on the part of the learner, even the most articulate, eloquent presentation will not fulfill its goal. This further pinpoints the importance of practicality in our programs. Your participants have every right to be told *why* this particular topic or session is included and *why* they are expected to learn this skill, knowledge, or attitude. Without this information, it may be difficult for some trainees to recognize the value of a session or to prepare themselves for learning.

*Orientation to learning.* While there may be some training sessions where the memorization of facts and figures is critical, certainly the majority of training situations call for "real world" attitudes and values. Case studies or role-play techniques allow the participants to "plug in" to realistic problems. Learning is best when this closeness to the actual job or task is apparent. Transfer of learning, likewise, will also be easier when this ready application to real problems can be shown to the learner. Remember, children are usually "taught" with a teacher-centered approach; adults are best "taught" with a real-world approach.

An even newer term, *synergogy,* is the creation of Robert Blake and Jane Srygley Mouton of Management Grid fame. Synergogy describes a new approach to HRD that claims to enhance motivation, learning, and retention. Its derivation, *synergos,* that is, working together, and *agogus,* referring to "leader of" or teacher, means "working together for shared teaching."

Blake and Mouton posit that synergogy is different from other theories in three ways:

1. It offers meaningful direction through learning designs and instruments.

2. It relies on a team rather than an individual or group.

3. It is based on synergogy, that is, the whole can be more than the sum of its parts.

## LAWS OF LEARNING

Textbooks on educational psychology are often filled with dozens of laws of learning. Rather than reiterate them, let's discuss those few that are directly relevant to your responsibilities.

*The law of effect.* This law states that people learn best in pleasant surroundings. Adult learners are more likely to accept and repeat those activities and responses that are pleasant and satisfying to them. Think about this in physical terms as well as psychological ones. Look at your own organization's training facilities. Comfortable furniture (tables and chairs) in a warm, pleasant environment will do much to aid the learning process. Conversely, a training room filled with tablet arm chairs may actually detract from effective learning. For some, the staid rows of tablet arm chairs may be an unpleasant reminder of a less-than-satisfactory school or college experience. Moreover, an attitude of unpleasantness or an air of hostility sensed by participants will definitely hamper the learning process. A pat on the back for a trainee after a particular task or activity is an excellent way to practice the law of effect.

*The law of exercise.* Remember how you first learned your arithmetic tables . . . 2 times 2 equals 4; 3 times 2 equals 6; and so on? Well, you were learning them by "overlearning," that is, by doing something over and over and over again. This is what the law of exercise is all about. Think back to how you learned to ride a bicycle. With the helping hand of a parent or older friend, you learned to ride a bike by *riding* that bike—the redundant activity of trying again and again until you mastered the coordination necessary to complete that learning activity.

We know that retention is highest with participant involvement. The law of exercise recognizes this principle and suggests you involve your learners as much as possible, consistent with the time and goals of your session.

"Practice makes perfect" is another maxim of this law. This assumes that the practice or activity is the correct action to begin with. There are times when you may have to "unlearn" an improper method or incorrect exercise prior to learning the right way. Any reader who has been in the military service can recall the way in which firearms training was conducted. Considerable time is typically spent in "unlearning" the usual way of pulling the trigger and then more time is spent in teaching one to "squeeze" the trigger. This same analogy holds in our own training activities. If you are teaching a skill, you will want to be certain that previous patterns or earlier actions are in line with your desired outcomes. If not, you will want to correct those psychomotor skills before attempting to develop the new activity.

*The law of readiness.* Research clearly shows that adults can—and will— learn when the need to know is there. In other words, you will learn when you feel it is important to know more about a particular skill, knowledge, or attitude. Simplistic as this may appear to you, it is a proven truism in adult learning theory. When a person senses that need to know, the motivation and readiness are there and your task becomes that much easier. If we can show the trainee why the content is important and relate the immediacy of its application to the job situation, we can put the learner in a readiness position.

*The law of association.* This is a basic foundation of all of our learning activities. It essentially means that every new fact, idea, or concept is best learned if we can relate it to already known information. Learning can be likened to a series of children's building blocks where each new block is added to the existing set: we literally add each new bit of information to our existing body of information. If the new "block" of information can be related or associated to already known information, long-term learning is more easily assured. For example, as you hear someone tell a story or anecdote, you may be reminded of a similar story or experience. Association is the basis of much of our learning. We are often conditioned to items through subtle means of association. For example, through association of colors, a green traffic light means "go"; the red traffic light "tells" us to stop.

The more we can build on earlier experiences or knowledge, the better our training effort becomes. As in any kind of educational process, our task is to guide people from "where they are" to "where you want them to be." After all, this is the change in behavior we identify as "learning."

## UNDERLYING PRINCIPLES

In addition to these basic laws of learning, there are several other principles that will help us better understand how adults learn.

*Learning is a self-activity.* The accumulation of knowledge, skills, and attitudes is an experience that occurs within the learner and is really activated by the learner. While we as trainers can set the stage and do much to orchestrate a climate conducive to learning, it is an internal process. One of the richest resources for learning is the learners themselves, and the learning process may be different for each of them. For this reason, human resource developers must recognize and respect the individuality of the trainees.

*We learn at different rates.* We all have "good" days and "bad" days. It is perfectly natural to experience some "ups and downs" in the learning process. Although one might expect that tomorrow's performance or learning achievements should always be better than yesterday's, things don't always turn out that way! While we may observe a ready and enthusiastic early rate of learning, it might be unrealistic to expect a steady marked increase throughout every successive session. Psychological as well as physiological factors can curtail effective learning. These "learning plateaus"—so called because the skill or knowledge may seem to taper off and even regress— are commonly observed in many training situations. Unfortunately, most trainees don't know this, so it is important for us to step in quickly with a word of encouragement during these "off days." Reassurance and empathy are key elements in this task.

*Learning is a continuing and a continual process.* We hear more and more about the term *continuing education.* Indeed, we must be vocal proponents of this lifelong process. Moreover, we should be living examples of this principle by being continuous learners ourselves. This does not necessarily refer to an academic setting; on the contrary, the astute and observant trainer can always be learning from colleagues and trainees.

*Learning results from stimulation to the senses.* This is probably a familiar one. Your trainees will learn better when you can appeal to all their senses. This premise substantiates the need for visuals to reinforce your session. In studies of how people learn and how they forget, estimates indicate that we can increase learning threefold by letting them *see* rather than only letting them *hear.* By practicing the age-old "show and tell" concept, we can dramatically increase the resultant learning. The more we can involve the learner with "hands-on" experiences, the better the learning is. Retention, too, is by far enhanced with greater use of the senses.

*Positive reinforcement enhances learning.* Your participants will more likely repeat those activities wherein a positive reinforcement occurred. Credit and recognition will provide a rich incentive for learning. Trainees will repeat those behavior patterns that may be accompanied by a feeling of self-esteem. It could be claimed that we are all concerned about increasing our own potential as people. When we are given that nod of encouragement or the verbal pat on the back for a task well done, we generally have a good feeling toward ourselves and the situation in general. Admittedly a controversial area among senior trainers, reinforcement theory *does* have its place in the HRD arena.

*We learn best by doing.* This principle is closely related to earlier items. If you want your participants to really learn to perform a task, have them actually *do* the task. The use of on-the-job training techniques clearly proves its value. The "learn-by-doing" concept will enable your trainees to garner self-confidence since they can show you—and themselves—that they can satisfactorily perform the prescribed tasks. Research tells us that the most effective learning results when the initial training is followed immediately by an application process. The more similar this application is to the actual job situation, the better the long-term learning.

*"Whole-part-whole" learning is best.* This is an important concept to follow. It means that we start the training process by looking first at the "big picture," or the entire job. After discussion of the total picture, making sure there is complete understanding, we break down the task into its component parts and show how each piece fits into the puzzle. Individual parts of a job should be explained in detail only after your participants understand the overall job. For example, in an orientation session for new employees, it is preferable to describe or explain the company or organization in total before describing the respective job in particular. By so doing, you show the new employees where their duties fit into the overall picture of the organization. If they know how a particular department relates to other offices or departments, the employees gain a better appreciation of how it all fits together.

So, too, with learning a new skill. Start with the complete process—the whole job. Then follow up describing how the individual intricate parts come together to make that whole.

*Anxieties and nervousness are natural.* Many of us approach a new task or a new activity with innate fears, preconceptions, and a general feeling of nervousness. Empathy and understanding of these frustrations will help the trainee feel more at ease.

Consider using "climate-setting" activities or ice-breakers to ease these tensions. They'll work to ease the trainees' (and the trainers'!) anxieties.

*Training must be properly timed.* Several short training periods are more effective than one long session. Whenever possible or practical, "spaced" learning is preferred over concentrated sessions.

Obviously there are times when these intermittent sessions are simply not practical or possible. Perhaps because of time and travel costs, the training must be concentrated. For these situations, use a variety of teaching techniques and participative exercises to change the pace of training.

## APPLYING THE PRINCIPLES

It does little good to memorize a few theories or principles of learning if we cannot apply them directly to our field of human resource development.

As a new trainer, you will be comforted to know that there are many ways in which you can use the basic laws of learning to enhance your effectiveness in the training room. For example, you help establish the climate in your own sessions. A warm, friendly atmosphere, as suggested by the law of effect, will provide a congenial yet businesslike environment. Similarly, by realizing that "practice *may* make perfect," as shown by the law of exercise, we can make certain that the activity is learned correctly. By rewarding or praising the new trainee after successful completion of the tasks being taught, you further reinforce the proper action.

Knowing that learning is a self-activity should not be used as a copout. Merely because the law of readiness states there must be the internalized desire to learn, we cannot shirk our own responsibility as trainer. Your professional responsibility is to help cause that change in behavior we call "learning."

Because we know that we construct our body of knowledge much like a child builds with toy blocks, we go from the simple to the complex. The law of association is useful as we write out our lesson plans and design our training programs. Learning is based on past experiences, and early successes will help the trainee maintain interest and enthusiasm for the training effort.

Regardless of the kind of training or training program in which you are involved, these fundamental principles will apply to you and your participants.

## SUMMARY

This brief overview of the principles of learning and their application is only the tip of the proverbial iceberg. In an attempt to keep this volume usable and practical, we have had to exclude many of the recognized theorists of adult learning. Serious students of learning theory are advised to continue independently by referring to the bibliography in this book.

The few laws and principles identified in this chapter have been proven to be useful to our field. By mastering and practicing these, you are already well on your way to being an effective facilitator for learning.

# CHAPTER 11

# Motivation

*If the learner hasn't learned, the teacher hasn't taught.*

How would you respond to that statement?

We would be surprised if there is any initial disagreement with that opening sentence. Certainly, one could argue that if the learner did not learn anything, then it must be obvious the teacher did not teach.

But is it really a truism? We think not.

Perhaps nothing could stir as much controversy—even among experienced trainers—as does our beginning premise. This chapter may begin to change your thinking—or at least let you raise some valid arguments on either side of the discussion.

We will also explore some of the more commonly accepted theories of motivation and show their direct application to the training function. Finally, you will be given several ideas that will help you better understand the nature of motivation and some workable methods to assist you in motivating your own participants.

## WHAT IS MOTIVATION?

Learning, like any human endeavor, is enhanced or attenuated by each person's internal motivations. Each of us has a wide range of needs that seek satisfaction. These needs, while vying for satisfaction, excite the drive or motive that determines our behavior. The need that is least satisfied dominates our behavior at that time.

Let's look at the word *motivation* and see precisely what it means. Managers and supervisors probably spend more time and effort in their attempts to motivate than in any other managerial function. And yet, the word—*motivation*—is often misused and very often misunderstood by many of us.

Our definition comes straight from the dictionary: "That within the individual, rather than without, which incites him to action. Any need, idea, emotion, or organic state that prompts an action."

## MOTIVATION, BEHAVIOR, AND NEEDS

The old argument about motivation being internal or external can be easily resolved. Motivation is 100-percent internal. It is the immediate pressing drive resulting from the internal tension that occurs when a need has not been satisfied. No external action can extinguish the desire for the satisfaction of that need, even though an external action may affect the way you behave (the action you take).

So, it's not *motivation* that's affected by external actions—it's *behavior*. Both camps can win the argument if they agree on basic definitions. Motivation is internal, while behavior is affected by both internal and external pressures.

## HOW TO MOTIVATE

It is generally acknowledged that there is really only *one* way to make anybody do anything. Did you ever really think about that?

As you do so, you will come to realize that there is, indeed, only one way that you can motivate your trainees, your colleagues, or your subordinates to ever do anything. The answer is all too simple—you must make them *want* to do it. There is no other way.

Carrying this premise a bit further, we could continue by stating that there are two general ways to make that person *want* to do something. The first, which is the better of the two, is the positive approach. It suggests that people may be motivated to gain an increase in satisfaction. It says merely that our participants—and everyone else—react better in a friendly atmosphere.

The second method, while workable, should be used sparingly. It essentially states that people may be motivated to do things to avoid a decrease in satisfaction. People may be motivated through fear or danger. This approach should be used only when all efforts at positive motivation fail.

## THE NATURE OF MOTIVATION

What we have said so far may be paraphrased simply by stating that to learn, we must want to learn. Without that basic desire on the part of the trainee, it is extremely difficult for even the most articulate trainer to force learning. It is all but impossible in today's society to force anyone to perform tasks he or she simply does not want to do.

In learning, the want and need for instruction must be recognized and acknowledged. As we discussed in an earlier chapter, learning is the process of changing behavior so that these wants and needs can be satisfied or achieved. In all learning, the person must want to learn.

In training sessions in which attendance is voluntary, the trainer may tend to assume that the attendees have recognized the need and that the want—and motivation—are already there. In those sessions your participants have to attend, the picture, of course, is completely different. Your task, then, is to change the attitudes of a person or a group to a positive one first. This, of course, is easier said than done. But by using the techniques outlined in this chapter, you can make your job easier.

## THEORIES OF MOTIVATION

Of the hundreds of studies conducted in the field of motivation, we shall discuss only a few that seem to have the most direct application in the field of human resource development. Let's review these five:

Western Electric Studies

Theory X and Theory Y

Maslow's Hierarchy of Needs

Skinner's Behavior Modification

Expectancy Theory

### Western Electric Studies

One of the most quoted studies in motivation and human relations was conducted in the late 1920s at the Hawthorne works of the Western Electric Company near Chicago, Illinois.

After doing some preliminary investigations regarding the effect of illumination on productivity, a team of industrial psychologists entered this plant and picked six women to continue as the control group in a new series of experiments. Several techniques were tried on this control group to determine how they would affect productivity.

A special effort was made to encourage the cooperation of the women. They were even consulted before any of the conditions were altered. The hope, of course, was to show that if free communications between worker and management were encouraged, mutual respect would follow.

Initially, rest periods were introduced. Productivity increased. And oddly, no matter what the length of the break, output continued to increase.

A piecework program was then initiated. This, too, was greeted by an increase in productivity. Changes were then made in the length of the work day. Even with a *decrease* in the number of work hours, output increased.

On the surface, it would appear that rest periods, piecework, and shorter hours might increase productivity. To further validate the findings, the team began to remove the conditions. The rest periods were eliminated. Longer work hours were restored. The piecework rate was replaced by a straight salary. The result? Increased output in every case!

What could have caused this? What made this group of women different from their coworkers is that they were made to feel as if they were "something special." Being chosen for the test gave these people a feeling of importance.

This conclusion was further supported in over 20,000 interviews. When instilled with a feeling of importance, workers were willing to cooperate. If, on the other hand, they were merely "numbers" to management, there was no reason for *wanting* to cooperate.

So what does all this mean to you as you go about your responsibilities in training? The most important thing to remember is that you can build an "esprit de corps" in all of your classes and sessions by recognizing the individuality and the importance of each person. The team effort so necessary in any organization is equally important with any group. Recognize that all these people, regardless of background or experience (or lack of it), are important to you as well as to themselves. Your role, especially for the trainee who might feel out of place or less than adequate, is critical. Help that person become part of the team and your effort will be a truly rewarding one.

### Theory X and Theory Y

Another classic study was undertaken by the late Douglas Murray McGregor of the Massachusetts Institute of Technology. He described two theories of management and their implications for motivation: Theory X and Theory Y.

McGregor's Theory X basically has five premises: (1) Most people, by nature, don't like to work. (2) Most people lack ambition and need a club over their heads in order to make them work. (3) Most people prefer to be told what to do. (4) Most people resist change. (5) Most people are gullible and not overly intelligent.

Theory Y, on the other hand, is more "people oriented" and has four cornerstones: (1) People do not dislike work but may actively seek it. (2) People do not need the authoritative type of leadership but prefer a participative kind of management. (3) People prefer setting their own goals rather than have someone else set them. (4) People do not shirk responsibility but rather seek it.

It is evident that Theory X and Theory Y have conflicting and contradictory points of view. The studies show that Theory X, the task-centered approach, may be effective in some cases, but that Theory Y, the people-centered approach, is likely to be more effective.

The relevance for human resources is readily apparent. By definition, we are in the people business. While the task (training activity) is crucial, we must always temper it with the Theory Y approach. Classroom and training facility conditions should be provided to allow for individuals to develop at their own rate and to help them set their own training objectives.

## Maslow's Hierarchy of Needs

A concise and interesting framework of workable ideas is offered by Professor Abraham H. Maslow. In his well-known and operational hierarchy of needs, he views an individual's motives in a priority ranking. As the needs of a lower level are satisfied, others quickly become apparent. A completely satisfied need is not a motivator. For example, take the air we breathe. Unless we are deprived of it, we don't even think about it. By the same token, when starvation is impending, you could care little about higher needs!

It is recognized that each of us has certain basic needs in any kind of social organization. What are these needs? How can we as trainers help our participants satisfy them?

Maslow's hierarchy of needs includes (1) physiological needs, (2) safety and security needs, (3) social needs, (4) esteem and self-respect needs, and (5) self-realization needs.

**Physiological needs** First and foremost in the priority of needs are the biological and physiological things that we need to survive. These are the basic drives, including the needs for food, rest, drink, and shelter.

**Safety and security needs** When the first-level needs are largely satisfied, the next level comes into play. These needs include freedom from fear, danger, threats, and so forth. If we encounter certain policies that arouse fear or uncertainty, these needs may become powerful motivators.

**Social needs** When we are no longer fearful about the first two levels, our social needs begin to surface. The need for belonging and for peer acceptance is important to us. We want to give—and to receive—friendship.

**Esteem and self-respect needs** Personal recognition—personal wealth and self-esteem—is the fourth item in the hierarchy of needs. The pat on the back for a job well done or the word of praise given in the presence of others are important methods of fulfilling this need. These are sometimes called the ego or status needs.

**Self-realization** A capstone of our needs is self-actualization. The basic need of self-fulfillment is one that few ever really satisfy. It can be a constant motivator, since most people will never fully attain it. However, the need to "keep trying" nudges us to keep moving toward that goal.

The implications of this important theory are both many and varied. Let's review each of the five basic needs and show how they apply to the training area:

*Physiological.* The basic physical conditions of your training rooms will help or hinder the learning process. For example, the types of chairs and/or tables, the lighting, the room temperature, and the decor of the room are but a few items that play a subtle role in motivation. See that facilities are as good as you can make them.

*Safety and security.* In addition to the obvious factors of safety, there are other equally important things to consider. For example, students who feel insecure will fail to participate, avoid risks, and keep low profiles. They don't take chances so that they won't get into trouble. If they know the ground rules and expectations of the program, this fear can be allayed.

Give a word of praise for a job well done. Provide reasonable opportunities for the students to talk over their special problems with you.

*Social.* By making the new attendee a part of the group, we're offering a basic satisfaction. The office cliques that carry on into the conference room may be fine for its established members, but how about the newcomer?

Students who feel they are not accepted members of the group will try to gain group identification by conforming to group standards. They'll speak up and participate but only in agreement with group-supported issues. Their actions are guided by their motivation to win group acceptance.

*Esteem.* The drive for recognition, status, and prestige can be fulfilled with a kind word or a compliment given in front of the group. The motive for recognition directs behavior. Esteem needs may be exhibited by active participation in group discussions or continued attempts at subgroup leadership. For some, this satisfaction may be internalized; for others, it must be overt.

Call students by name. Let them work in groups occasionally. Find ways of appropriately recognizing good achievement. Use their exhibits and displays of outstanding work.

*Self-actualization.* People motivated by self-realization are seeking and usually attain a sense of accomplishment. Motivated by challenges, new systems, and new methods, these individuals often perform in a creative way. They are growth oriented and seek new tasks and positive feedback on past performance.

Remember, a learning climate must be established at the outset and reaffirmed continuously.

## Skinner's Behavior Modification

B. F. Skinner's work with learning theory is a classic. Behavior modification is a type of reinforcement that recognizes and rewards positive actions or behavioral patterns. We know from learning theory that people tend to repeat those activities that are pleasant and satisfying. Positive reinforcement, as practiced by a word of encouragement, a verbal pat on the back, or some other act of affirmation subtly tells the employees or the trainees that their work is good. The motivation, of course, through these positive types of reinforcement, provides the climate that prompts and encourages repetition of these patterns of behavior.

As a corollary of positive reinforcement, negative reinforcement is in evidence when the behavior pattern is coupled with the removal of a negative consequence. It is important to note that this is not to be equated with punishment, because in reprimands or other negative tools something unpleasant or unfavorable usually results.

**How Positive Reinforcement Works** As indicated previously, reinforcement theory—in its simplest form—says that if a behavior is rewarded it will reoccur. If ignored, it will become extinct and, if punished, it will cease for the immediate term but may cause undesirable side effects.

A positive reinforcer is a stimulus that provides a feeling of satisfaction or pleasure. If the feeling occurs immediately after a specific behavior and is perceived as resulting from that behavior, then the behavior is reinforced as being an appropriate way to act. People who receive positive reinforcement for their behavior will repeat that behavior in an effort to reexperience the pleasure or satisfaction.

**How to Apply Positive Reinforcement in Training** There are two ways to apply positive reinforcement to reward desirable behavior or learning—*pairing* and *shaping*. Pairing is used when the specific desirable behavior occurs and shaping is used when a close approximation of the desired behavior occurs.

*Pairing.* When a pleasure-evoking stimulus occurs simultaneously with or immediately after a certain behavior, the stimulus and the behavior are said to be paired. The stimulus could be the satisfaction from eating, sleeping, drinking, swimming, or any mental or emotional activity. The implications for training are that you can reinforce learning by pairing a positive reinforcer with a learned behavior. You can provide rewards such as a smile, an affirmative nod of the head, cheerful comments and actions, attention, and recognition through questioning and feedback.

**115**

*Shaping.* Shaping is more difficult and takes more time. The same principle applies in that a positive reinforcer is provided to reinforce behavior. In this case, however, you are working with an approximation of the desired behavior.

When the student expresses a behavior that is close to the desired behavior, you reward that behavior with a mild reinforcer. As the student exhibits behavior closer and closer to the desired behavior, the reinforcing stimulus is increased. Slowly, step by step, you guide the student to the desired behavior.

**Cautions** You must carefully observe the students' reactions to the positive stimuli that you provide. Each person is different, and the same stimuli may not evoke pleasure or satisfaction from all students. When proper stimuli are provided, the students' expressions will reveal their pleasure.

Another problem to watch for is the simultaneous occurrence of complicating stimuli. If other stimuli are perceived by the students as negative, they may be more influenced by the negative stimuli, especially if it comes from their peers. In this case, try to provide additional positive stimuli so that, on balance, the students perceive the situation as rewarding.

One final caution—a reinforcing stimulus that is used over and over or a reinforcement that is continually used for a specific behavior becomes predictable to the students. Once a predictable pattern is established, the reinforcement loses its impact. In order to avoid this situation, vary the reward and use it intermittently.

### Expectancy Theory

The expectancy model was initially developed by Victor H. Vroom, but it has since been given many names and attracted many followers. The *self-fulfilling prophecy* and the *Pygmalion effect* are two terms very much in vogue.

Vroom suggests that motivation is directly correlated to how much we want something and the probability that certain activities and actions will lead to obtaining it. The strength of an individual's belief that *something* will lead to something *else* is what's called an *expectancy*. As one builds and mentally imagines an outcome, the expectancy is that one can make it happen.

Success stories of star athletes who have achieved their stardom through mental imagery are legend. The same can be true for trainers.

Informal research indicates clearly that the expectations of a teacher or trainer definitely affect the behavior of the learner. In other words, if a trainer believes the room is full of lazy, passive, and inarticulate people, the group is so treated and will probably perform accordingly. Conversely, if you walk into a room knowing your group is alive, vibrant, and enthusiastic, more often than not, this is what you will end up having! A basic fact of human behavior is that people will tend to play the roles and act out the behavior patterns expected of them. Remember this, and your sessions will be that much better!

## THE PRACTICALITY OF SUBCONSCIOUS MOTIVES

Fortunately, most of our motives are subconscious. We generally act to fulfill our needs without being aware that everything we do, every action we take, is the result of some motive. As Maslow said, "All behavior is motivated."

If we were consciously aware of all our needs, we would not be able to think logically or function smoothly. As we began to formulate a thought about the use of reinforcement in training, for example, our thought would be deflected by a thought about sticking with secure techniques and only those with which we feel comfortable. This thought would not be completed either—it might be deflected by a thought to gain recognition, which would be deflected by . . . and so on indefinitely.

So the suppression of our motives to our subconscious level permits us to keep our thoughts and actions clear, logical, and structurally sound. We are able to function efficiently without considering the hundreds of motives that might be directing our behavior.

## HOW TO DETERMINE WHAT PEOPLE'S MOTIVES ARE

It is much easier to recognize other people's motives than our own. The verbal and physical actions of people provide us with and draw our attention to specific behavior that we can analyze and evaluate. There are two specific types of techniques that you can use to determine people's motives—observational techniques and listening techniques.

### Observation Techniques

Just as you recognize that people are nervous, anxious, or bored when they tap their fingers, so, too, can you determine their motives by observing their behavior over a period of time. Since behavior is often the result of a complex array of motives, you can't identify motives with complete accuracy, but you can make inferences from observed behavior. You can watch the things people do and the actions they take and infer with reasonable accuracy what motive incited the action.

If you see that a particular person consistently avoids the limelight, tries to keep a low profile, does very little talking, withholds information, expresses more than normal doubts, avoids new undertakings and risks, and generally tries to stick with the tried and true, you may infer that this person is motivated by security. Any action that is taken to keep out of trouble or give a safe feeling is generally motivated by security.

A person who is overly friendly, who participates openly in discussions, and who joins groups, clubs, and sports teams is generally motivated by social needs. People who seek office, high class standing, and high grades, and who try to gain status or recognition for their achievements, may be motivated by prestige needs.

Finally, the self-actualizing person will be trying new things and will be attracted to subject matter from a wide variety of fields. This person will participate to learn, to find new challenges, and to increase personal competence in every area. The self-actualizing person will be helpful to others without being pedantic or domineering.

By carefully observing people's behavior, you can often determine the motives that dominate that behavior. Remember that the most deprived need that a person has will be the dominating motive. If you know that someone has recently lost a job, for example, you may expect most of that person's behavior to be security oriented.

### Listening Techniques

Most people are poor listeners. One reason for poor listening habits is that as we listen we generally are evaluating what people say to determine whether or not we are being misled. We are on guard against people who may try to trick, fool, or manipulate us. These habits may be valuable protectors, but they may also cause us to miss valuable information.

In determining people's motives, the traditional way of defensive listening must be put aside. You must take an exploratory approach rather than an evaluative one.

### HOW TO TRIGGER THE DESIRE TO LEARN

To initiate the desire to learn, you must relate the content of your training program to one or more motives of your trainees. Research has shown that employees do not always see the relationship between their job assignments and their own personal goals. This may be because they are not consciously aware of their motives.

You can evoke a partial awareness of the underlying motives by stating and thus reminding a trainee that a specific action (learning a specific skill) will fulfill an acknowledged need. Your influence, then, in triggering the desire to learn is to remind the trainee how the course content will fulfill job needs for competence and personal needs for security, affiliation, esteem, and self-realization. You do this by mentioning a specific benefit—one that relates to a specific need that will result from learning the course content or the job skill.

### Relating Benefits to Job Needs

If employees can see how learning a new skill or behavior will help on the job, the internal motivational drives will take over. Employees will be internally directed or motivated to learn the skill in order to achieve the job goal. By *reminding* them or making them aware that the training activity will fulfill specific needs, you will trigger an internal motivation to learn.

Job needs are those that are tangible and specific in nature. People are usually aware of them and are willing to discuss them. Through class discussion you may get the participants to develop a list. This list of job needs then becomes your target. You relate the various elements of the training program to this list and thus influence the class members' motivation to learn.

The following list of job needs is typical of the list that a group may generate when asked to do so:

*Job needs*

Doing a good job

Adequate salary

Promotions

Salary increase

Easier work

Lack of confusion on the job

Titles commensurate with responsibility

Fair treatment

Equal opportunities

Good working conditions

Interesting work

Security

Recognition

Feeling of belonging

To trigger the internal drives that create the desire to learn, again, all you really have to do is remind members of the class that a particular bit of knowledge or skill will help them achieve their job needs. You might say, for example: "Learning how our company policy applies to receiving and distributing raw materials will *eliminate confusion on the job.*" All of those participants who have felt confused in this area will be internally motivated to learn the policy.

When dealing with one person, a single reference to a single job need will usually be sufficient. In a class, however, a number of references or *reminders* must be used in order to appeal to the needs of the entire class. You may do this by relating one element of the training function to a number of the job needs and/or by relating different elements of the training program to different job needs.

### Relating Benefits to Personal Needs

Relating training benefits to personal needs is no different from relating them to job needs. In both cases you are *reminding* the participants that the training will fulfill a need. Since personal needs are often unconscious, you must first bring them into awareness.

A small group or total class discussion could be used to do this. As the group members discuss what personal needs are, they will come to the realization that many of these needs are their own. At the very least, they will realize that the needs apply to people in general.

Let the class or subgroups develop a list of personal needs immediately after the discussion. By the end of this activity, many trainees will have experienced an "aha!" feeling of enlightenment. They will see that some of their own personal needs are being discussed. The following is a representative list of the personal needs that may evolve.

*Personal needs*

A sense of accomplishment

An opportunity to grow

A feeling of pride

Recognition for ability and efforts

A voice in decisions that affect me

Authority

Honest praise

Time to socialize

Being in the know

Being comfortable in associations and tasks

Security

Friendship and approval

Lack of worry

Lack of risks

Lack of embarrassment

Knowledge of the environment

Again, all you need to do to initiate the internal motives to fulfill these needs is to pick out an element in your training program, match it to one or more of these needs, and remind the participants that the learning will fulfill those needs. Then their internal drives will be triggered into action and your training will become easier.

## SUMMARY

All of us as human resource developers must continually increase our understanding of human behavior and human motivation. By so doing, we become more effective in our training responsibilities.

People, regardless of age or background, can learn if they *want* to learn. We can help by establishing an atmosphere conducive to the learning process. Because motivation is internal, it may be difficult to judge motives. We realize that all behavior is caused and a person will change behavior according to wants or needs at the time. Our function, of course, is to understand and acknowledge those needs and channel them into the correct learning climate.

## CHAPTER 12

# Facilitation Skills

*"We can't teach anyone. What we do is facilitate learning . . ."*

**Carl Rogers**

Let's begin by explaining what we mean by the role of facilitation. Although its use is becoming increasingly popular among HRD professionals, it is not always uniformly understood.

A facilitative role is quite different from that of a traditional teacher role. Let's compare and contrast some of the differences:

|                  *Teacher*            |                   *Facilitator*                |
| ------------------------------------- | ---------------------------------------------- |
| ● Presents information                | ● Guides discussion                            |
| ● Provides the right answers          | ● Provides the right questions                 |
| ● One-way communication               | ● Two-way communication                        |
| ● Gives assignments                   | ● Coordinates learning activities              |
| ● Dictates objectives                 | ● Melds group's goals                          |
| ● Teacher-centered                    | ● Learner-centered                             |

As you can begin to see, the facilitator's role is considerably different from that of the teachers (or trainers!) you have known.

The facilitator fully understands and practices the learner-centered mode of presenting information. A skillful and attentive listener, he or she has mastered the art of questioning and guides the group toward their mutually agreed upon objectives. Knowing the group's needs and interests, the facilitator adroitly uses the group's experiences to help them learn. Quickly established as a team member, he or she still maintains a subtle control over the participants.

As you probably now agree, the facilitator is a very special kind of trainer. By providing a variety of learning experiences, the facilitator creates a climate conducive to effective training. Even though the facilitator has the answers, questions are ricocheted back to the group. So much for background; let's get started.

## FACILITATE

As you progress from novice to seasoned trainer, you will begin to see that facilitation is a key skill for the professional. The professional trainer must learn to manage the entire range of elements that make up the training program. We learn, for example, to use questions to facilitate and to deal with difficult trainees in a constructive rather than destructive way. This chapter provides the basis for learning these group facilitation skills.

## GETTING A GOOD START

It is important to begin a session in a way that creates a good climate and develops interest. The following ideas will help you set the stage and keep interest and attention throughout the session.

*Be prepared.* In addition to being prepared to make a presentation, you must also make sure all your materials are on location in their proper place and in proper order. You should arrive at the class location at least an hour before the session starts. This will give you time to check the room and your materials, and still have time to review your presentation.

*Build interest from the first minute.* People are interested in other people as well as themselves. One way to develop interest is to tell the group about yourself and then ask each of them to tell about themselves. Other variations are mentioned earlier in this book.

*Use case studies.* The use of case studies is an excellent way to develop interest. People can get involved in using the skills you are teaching to solve the case. Make sure the case is relevant to the material so that the trainees can see the value of the ideas and skills you are teaching.

*Keep the training on the track.* The session should move at a pace rapid enough to hold interest. Time should be allowed for the material to sink in but not so much that the group gets sidetracked with other topics. Extraneous conversation within the group indicates it's time to move on.

*Change the pace.* You can keep interest high by changing back and forth between discussion, case study, problem solving, work activities, or personal presentations by the trainees.

*Ask for questions.* Allow time for questions after each major point. Present an idea, discuss it, provide an exercise to use it, and ask for questions. Many people will let you move to a new point before they understand the material unless you specifically ask for questions.

*Keep control.* Remember, you have a specific quantity of material to cover. Provide enough time in your schedule to cover each point thoroughly but be prepared to take control and move ahead if time is becoming a concern.

*Encourage humor.* In some sessions, humor may evolve naturally. If it's comfortable for you, encourage an informal atmosphere of humor. Humor relaxes the participants and enhances learning.

*Summarize.* Summarize each section of material before starting a new section. This not only enhances learning but also offers participants a final chance to question material they may have missed earlier.

*End on a high.* Save a new idea or important point to make at the end of the program. Make sure the summary recaps a few of the ideas presented, but still present something special the trainees can use and remember. If the program ends on a high note, the participants will look forward to the next program.

## CREATIVE QUESTIONING SKILLS

In the role of facilitator, the skill of asking questions is an important one. Questions are especially useful because they are learner-centered and ask the participant to think through the problem, analyze the question, or evaluate his or her behavior. Questioning, if done properly, can be used to control behavior by bringing the individual's own intellectual processes to bear on the situation.

### Why Ask Questions?

Many instructors complain that their participants seldom become completely involved in group activities. There are many reasons for this lack of involvement in class activities (including a dull or uninteresting presentation!). But the answer to correcting the problem may be found without analyzing all the causes. Although you may wish to determine causes for the purpose of improving the overall program, you may develop interest and participation by asking questions.

*Questioning encourages involvement by providing an opportunity for exchanging ideas and information.* One way that questioning encourages involvement is through the interest that participants develop in sharing their ideas. Once a question has been asked, participants in the group begin to think about the question and generate ideas. Different participants obviously have different ideas and may want to express them. They then attempt to get time to express these ideas and thus become involved in the program.

*Questioning elicits comments from the class, which enables the instructor to assess what the participants already know as well as what they need to learn.*

The participants, in answering questions, show the depth of their knowledge. Their comments and questions reveal those areas in which they are weak and give the instructor a better grasp of their needs. By making a few notes while a discussion is occurring in the class, the instructor can prepare additional comments to clarify any area of misunderstanding.

*Asking questions provides a way to arouse interest and create curiosity.* Not only do questions arouse interest by directing attention to a particular problem, but they also create curiosity. Very seldom do you find a question being dealt with on the basis of facts alone. Usually people express their feelings and opinions when answering questions. These feelings and opinions grew out of personal experiences. As feelings and opinions are expressed, curiosity develops on the part of the other participants and this results in additional comments and questions.

*Asking questions can be used to emphasize and reinforce the significant points of information presented.* By asking a question, you draw the person's attention to the point you are trying to make. You might ask, "How would you apply this in your own work?" Or, you could present the question "How would it work if you mixed this with the system you've been using?" You could ask for an evaluation of the principle expressed or a comparison of the new principle with one previously discussed. Any question that gets the participant to think through an application of the principle you are describing will emphasize that principle and enhance learning.

*Asking questions also teaches critical thinking.* Again, asking the students to compare, contrast, test, evaluate, and use the information you teach encourages critical thinking. One of the best applications of this principle is to pose a problem for the students to solve. In trying to solve the problem, they must think critically about the principle involved. If the problem is one that can be presented to the group to work on together, the participants get the benefit of seeing how the critical thinking skills of their peers are applied.

## TYPES OF QUESTIONS

Let's take a look at several different types of questions. You'll soon see how each or any of these might be employed to involve your participants.

*Direct questions.* This type of question is aimed at one person. For example, "John, what are some ways we can improve sales in this region?" Although it may elicit a response, it can also be dangerous in that the potential respondent may be embarrassed if he or she does not know the answer. Moreover, as soon as the instructor calls an individual by name, there is a natural tendency for other participants to stop listening; they may think, "Poor John, but at least I'm off the hook this time!"

*Indirect question.* As contrasted with the direct question, the indirect—or overhead—question is presented to the entire group. While the direct question is a rifle-type question, overhead questioning is often termed the "shotgun" approach because it involves all participants. For example, "What are a couple of ways we can increase sales?" is an indirect question. Hopefully, a quick response or two may be forthcoming. However, the experienced facilitator knows that quick responses may not necessarily follow! So be prepared. If there are no verbal responses, merely pause for a few seconds, then watch for a nonverbal cue that might suggest someone has an idea.

Incidentally, if you're a new trainer, we recommend that you seek out a friendly participant or two in advance and tell them you may call on them if no one else responds.

Experienced trainers agree that, once "the ice is broken," additional responses seem to flow much more easily.

*Factual questions.* These are closed-end questions and, while not recommended for continuing discussion, they can serve as a check on progress. "What's the number one reason people lose their jobs?" is a factual question. The typical answer, of course, is lack of interpersonal skills. Although some participants may discuss the pros or cons of the answer, it remains fairly academic.

*Attitude questions.* Strictly speaking, this type of inquiry is more of a subtle check on overall feelings or the pulse of the group. A "What do you think . . . ?" question evokes a response and, since there is no right or wrong answer, it encourages others to also comment.

*Double-check questions.* This approach allows the facilitator to assess participants' understanding. For example, "So what you mean is . . ." can very nicely confirm one's position. It is also a nonthreatening way to get feedback and make certain everyone is on the same wavelength.

*Assumptive questions.* Here is another good method to assist your participants in a positive way. By phrasing the question "You'll probably be using a flipchart for your practice session, won't you?", you're subtly suggesting that a flipchart should be used. Even if the person had not thought about it, he or she probably gets the hint that its use would enhance the practice session.

*Summary questions.* A final way to recap or review respective parts of the session, the summary question attempts to bring closure to a point. "So what we've agreed on is . . ." suggests that participants will agree or disagree to the extent required. It is an excellent tool with which the facilitator can determine if he or she is on target.

## SUMMARY

By definition, *facilitate* means "to make easier." Admittedly a rather simplistic approach, its application is far more difficult to practice. As this chapter illustrates, facilitation skills are quite different from the typical trainer's role. It is obviously learner-centered rather than trainer-centered. While it places responsibility for learning on the learner, the responsibility of the facilitator is of prime importance. Through artful questioning—and truly knowing the participants and responding to their needs—the entire learning process becomes more fruitful. The facilitation process is, of course, very group-oriented, and the trainer-oriented instructor may have difficulty in relinquishing overt control of the group. This is not necessary if proper questioning techniques are employed. Indeed, it is a skill that must be mastered by the master trainer. So, practice these skills and make the transition from teacher to facilitator a rewarding one for you and your participants.

# CHAPTER 13

# Presentation Skills

*Unaccustomed as I am. . . .*

In a recent well-publicized listing of all the fears of the American people, the number one fear was "speaking before a group." Not surprising to most of us, this fear is one to which we can probably all relate.

Certainly we all recognize the importance of a well-planned and well-presented training program. We are probably a little envious when we see and hear a seasoned trainer who seems to have the uncanny ability to keep the audience "sitting on the edge of their chairs" awaiting the speaker's next words.

"Gee," we fantasize, "I wish I could do that someday." Well, that "someday" could start *this* day if you're willing to put some effort into it.

The steps are simple ones, but that doesn't necessarily mean they are easy ones. If you're like most of us who never have taken a course in public speaking, don't worry. Many exciting platform personalities still confess to getting the "butterflies" and other similar "first-day jitters" that we've all experienced.

So, if we've established a comfort zone for you, let's get started. For ease of reference, we'll use the basic four-step approach of:

Preparing

Presenting

Participating

Summarizing

## PREPARING

In a word, *plan!* Don't be misled when you see the seemingly spontaneous "off the cuff" remarks made by veteran trainers. They've done their homework and prepared thoroughly. Probably, they have given the same session before—or have been in similar situations—and their words, gestures, and responses are now all but second nature. But make no mistake—when these same people started out, they very likely used the same approach we're suggesting.

Preparation covers a lot of territory. It's the first step and may well be the most important. Let's look at a few of the items that require our attention.

*Audience.* Who are you speaking to? What are their backgrounds? These are but two of the questions you'll want to consider. The pro is always inquisitive about his or her audience. If we've done a thorough job of needs analysis, we already know something about our group. The more we know them, the more easily we can tailor our remarks to their needs and interests. And yet, many of us have had the unfortunate experience of listening to a trainer or speaker who apparently didn't have the slightest idea to whom she or he was speaking! The result is often a waste of time for both trainer and trainee.

If you're giving a talk to an outside group, find out about the kinds of organizations they represent and what kinds of job responsibilities your audience has.

If all this sounds like a lot of work, it is! But the results you'll get will definitely make up for the time and effort expended.

*Interests.* The interests, wants, and needs of the group should in large part dictate the central message of the program. This does not necessarily imply that we cover only those things they want to hear. Empty platitudes and flattery are quickly detected by an audience. Don't use compliments unless they are few and sincere. But any presentation should be tailored to be relevant to those listening.

*Goals.* You'll recall that we discussed objectives in Chapter 4. Again, we're already ahead of the game. Make certain, however, that your goals are consistent with the trainees'. A session for a special conference, sales meeting, or any other type of training program must have some goal in mind.

*Visual aids.* Examples, illustrations, and statistics can all be emphasized and made more understandable by the use of visual aids. Visual aids also can highlight and summarize each point as it is made, as well as show the relationship of one point to another.

Properly used, visual aids can be very effective. People enjoy watching something besides the trainer. A visual presentation captures their eyes as well as their ears. The more attention a trainer can focus on the subject, the more successful the session will be.

If you're using visuals, it's imperative that you check and double-check

the projectors, slides, and transparencies. While visual aids may add a vibrant dimension to your program, the upside-down slide or the burned-out projection bulb can cause anguish and embarrassment. So be prepared.

Keep the illustrations as simple and as dramatic as possible. Don't try to cram too much material into each card or slide. Charts should be brief, showing only major comparisons. Line drawings should be bold and clear. If a complicated relationship is to be presented, do it in a series of illustrations, not just one. To summarize the major points of the session, words can be used as illustrations (so can brief sentences), but keep those words to a minimum. If the point can be condensed in a half-dozen words, those words are far more likely to be remembered by an audience than a half-dozen sentences of explanation.

*Everything else!* We could probably fill volumes with the myriad things that demand some advance checking and preparation. For example, the room in which your talk will be given must be checked beforehand. If it's in a local restaurant or hotel, a casual visit is very much in order. If your talk is scheduled for a different city, try to arrive the day before your scheduled presentation. With all due respect, printed hotel diagrams of meeting rooms may not precisely describe the actual room, seating configuration, or space requirements. Check it out in advance.

## PRESENTING THE MESSAGE

Comes the big day! If the previous steps of planning, organizing, and preparing have been followed, the presentation will be challenging and satisfying. There are still a few things, however, that must be considered to ensure a successful session. A few tasks are performed before you approach the podium; some are done as the speech is in progress. Let's look at them briefly.

*Notes.* Should I use notes? There is some disagreement on whether any speaker or trainer should refer to notes when making a presentation. One school of thought says we must be completely prepared for the talk and that the open use of notes admits lack of preparation. On the other hand, some feel that notes are obvious evidence of preparation, and we should not feel the least embarrassed to show and use them. Unless the trainer is an experienced orator, the second course is preferable. Certainly, most audiences know that no appearance is undertaken without preparation. Except for rare occasions, don't read from a prepared manuscript. By the same token, a totally memorized presentation may lack sincerity.

The recommended way to prepare the content of the talk is to use a basic outline. More experienced trainers reduce the outline to a list of major

ideas and subheads. Someone who fully knows the ideas he or she wants to express needs only to glance at the notes for a key word or phrase. If you feel more comfortable having your talk initially written out in full—fine. But the preferred way is then to reduce it to outline form. Many experienced speakers use 5″ × 8″ cards.

Don't pretend to be an extemporaneous speaker if you're not. Occasionally speakers try to give the impression they are talking completely "off the cuff" and will not let the audience see they are using notes. Often this works fine until the speaker loses his place or his train of thought. The fumbling that results embarrasses both speaker and audience. Don't be ashamed to use notes.

*The parts of a talk.* With some of the preliminaries out of the way, you're ready now to transfer your thoughts to an organized presentation. How does one go about putting all these ideas into some workable form? What organization is best? This story provides a clue: Many years ago a Southern minister was acclaimed an excellent speaker. Though his command of the language was weak, his sermons were unforgettable. When asked his technique for getting people to listen on Sunday mornings, his response was simple. "First I tell them what I'm going to tell them. Then I tell them. Then I tell them what I told them." Any speaker will do well to copy that method.

Briefly, then, there are three parts to a presentation: (1) the introduction, (2) the body, and (3) the conclusion or summary. Leave out any part and the message is not complete.

1. The Introduction. The initial part of your session is a brief opening to capture the audience's attention. The introduction may be a humorous anecdote, a severe challenge, a serious question, or anything else to capture the interest of the group. The introduction also usually includes a brief preview of the program. Essentially, what is it that's in the message? What is the purpose of being there? What will the people in attendance gain? In other words, what return on their investment of time and attention can you give them?

2. The Body. The central theme of your session unfolds in its body. Although a sneak preview has been given in the introduction, the detailed message is delivered now. Recall the initial purpose of your appearance, and start from there in planning the heart of the presentation. Follow this up with the major premises and subtopics. Make no attempt to categorize them; the sequence and order of importance will come naturally later. Review all of the points you have noted, then combine and group them into as few major points as possible. Keep in mind that no one will be able to remember more than a few points from

any speech. As we said earlier, make it easy on the audience by setting forth only three or four major ideas in one talk. After the major subheadings are set, back them up with outside experiences, readings, etc.

Thus, the body of the speech contains the meat of the speech—the setting forth of the subjects to be covered and the discussion of those subjects. This is where the informing or the inspiring of the audience takes place. To achieve that goal, you need to pick the right technique or combination of techniques in light of the particular subject, the audience, and the occasion.

3. The Summary. At this point your audience has been led through the entire message. Although it may seem redundant to repeat the major points, don't fail to do so. Repetition reinforces memory. If the audience was taking notes, you favor them by letting them catch a point or two they may have missed the first time. You might restate the purpose of the talk, review a few major points, and thank the audience for listening. At times, a speaker may abruptly finish with the summary before the audience even knows he or she is concluding. The actual words "in conclusion" or "to summarize" give the audience a clue that the speaker is ready to finish.

*Appearance.* For any business group, conservative dress is always in proper taste. This holds true for men or women speakers. It is obvious that the speaker's appearance should not be "louder" than the speaker. Dress for the occasion, but don't overdress.

*Stage fright.* If your nerves are jumping all over your body, things are normal. In fact, some experts even claim this is a healthy and helpful sign. It keeps one "up" for the appearance. Several professional speakers freely admit to "butterflies" in the stomach before luncheon and dinner speeches. The important thing is not the nervousness but rather how to channel it to proper advantage. In other words, we want the "butterflies to fly in formation." For some people, engaging in social chitchat before the program takes their mind off the talk and minimizes nervousness. For others, concentration on the message, not the method, seems to relax the nerves.

In either case, nervousness can be minimized by first not becoming nervous at becoming nervous! A few short, deep breaths will help. Sit erect and don't slouch. A slouching position is not only offensive, but also pushes the stomach into the diaphragm and makes breathing more difficult. Another hint is to take two or three short breaths just before your session begins. This, too, cuts tension and helps one through the hardest part—the first few sentences of the talk.

*Humor.* Many public speaking handbooks suggest that humor is essential. Contrary to this popular belief, however, a speech does not have to be funny to be good; a speaker or trainer does not have to be a stand-up comedian or have a witty story for every example in order to be accepted by the audience. At the same time, the proper use of a humorous story or incident can do wonders in getting the audience to be responsive. Although a speaker may be correctly advised that "if they wanted entertainment, they would have hired a clown," most audiences like a spice of humor added to a talk. The use of an opening story, for example, is well accepted. But jokes and anecdotes should be used to illustrate a point or be relevant to the subject under discussion. This, in fact, should be a cardinal rule for all humor in public speaking. Tying the joke in with the message will not only make the point clearer but will also help the audience to remember it.

Many speakers feel that an occasional off-color story or profanity is all right and identifies the speaker as a person "who's with it." This is risky advice. The reason is simply that one can never fully know the audience and what may be a pleasant laugh to most might be very offensive to one person. The risk is just not worth it! Too many otherwise excellent trainers have been given sour receptions because of careless storytelling.

Audiences warm up quickly to good storytellers. Keep in mind, though, the overall purpose of the talk. If a person can amuse as well as inform, humor is an excellent technique for holding the attention and interest of the audience.

*Practicing.* No producer would ever dream of putting on a stage show without several rehearsals to check how well the actors play their roles. The same is true for a public speaker. While you can't have a dress rehearsal without a real audience, you still can use associates or perhaps family members as an audience.

If you are preparing the talk from an outline or a manuscript, reread the contents several times in order to become thoroughly familiar with them. Don't memorize, but obtain a good working knowledge of all the points being considered. If some parts seem awkward, reword them. Become completely natural with the tone and temper of the language. To be credible, a talk must reflect the speaker. Falseness is quickly detected by the listeners.

After the talk has been rewritten once or twice and words and phrases become familiar, it is time to get on with the show. A cassette recorder can be your best friend.

*Delivery.* When you practice the talk with a tape recorder, playback will reveal exactly what the audience would have heard had the speech been delivered that day. A recorder picks up all the "ahs" and "ers" and "you knows" a speaker uses. With a bit of conscious effort, these can be deleted.

It is better to be silent than use space fillers. Ah-ing and er-ing is an unfortunate habit that must be corrected if a speaker is to have the audience's full attention.

*Enthusiasm.* Deliver a message with a bubbling and vibrant presentation and people yearn to hear more. A sincere feeling of enthusiasm quickly draws out the same feeling from the crowd. The orator who solemnly reads page after page in a dull and dreary monotone deserves no audience and rarely gets one. With a little life and a spark of enthusiasm, your entire talk is enhanced. When a speaker says, "I'm glad to be here," people usually pass it off as a required part of the introduction. But when the speaker *shows* he's "glad to be here" by an exciting voice and friendly smile, people believe it. Vary the rate of speech, change inflection, and become charged up inside. You'll find enthusiasm a *must* in the delivery.

## PARTICIPATING

### *Get 'em involved.*

Communication is a two-way street. Your presentation will be more effective if you allow some kind of involvement or participation on the part of the listeners. If you want your audience to remember your talk, you'll do well to make some provision for them to be an active part of your session.

Adult learning theory suggests that retention is best when the learner is involved. That we learn by doing is a proven theory. Depending on the specific purpose or type of presentation you're giving, consider using some methods that will get the audience to take part in the program. While it is not the purpose of this section to describe the different techniques or methods available, consider such things as questions, discussion, buzz groups, or similar exercises.

Even if your time is limited and you can't employ some of these methods, you'll still get feedback. Watch for it. It may be nonverbal but will speak loudly if you catch it. The astute speaker is ever alert to these signals and will change the style or manner of presentation if so dictated by the participants.

## SUMMARIZING

As was indicated earlier, the summary is the last part of the talk. If there are several different parts to your talk, you may be well advised to summarize frequently throughout rather than do it all at the conclusion of your presentation.

This kind of review is a favor to your listeners. Rather than reiterate the major points in precisely the same words, a slight rewording or rephrasing is always in order.

Finally, a word about "thank yous." Some authors of public speaking books stress that speakers should never thank their audiences. This is strange and curious advice. It seems only common courtesy for a speaker to at least thank the audience for their attendance. If appropriate, certainlv a "thank you" for their interest and attention is also in order.

## A FINAL WORD

Before you grab your notes and start rushing off to anyone who will listen to you, you'll want to do some more homework and practice. Like any well-orchestrated production, the time and effort behind the scenes really make the difference in a polished product. So, too, with your speaking efforts. Lots of practice will perfect your style and delivery. Your local Toastmaster's Club is an excellent place to learn or brush up on these skills. If you've already been involved with Toastmasters, check into such groups as the National Speakers Association, an organization of both seasoned professionals and newcomers to the field.

# CHAPTER 14

# Planning a Meeting

*Whatever can go wrong—will!*

You've all heard of Murphy's Law. It is an ever-present possibility. (Incidentally, do you know what O'Toole's Law is? O'Toole says Murphy is an optimist!)

The field of meeting planning is a relatively new profession. Trainers can learn much from association and corporate meeting planners. Don't overlook hotel sales, convention, and catering staffs, as they can be extremely helpful in planning your off-site meetings.

In planning a training session, we can refer to the oft-used "five Ws" to remind us of certain factors that have real bearing on the effect of our sessions. They are:

*Who*—Who will be attending the training session?

*What*—What is the main topic to present? What are the stated objectives of my session?

*Where*—Where should the session be held?

*Why*—Why is this particular session included? Why are these participants attending?

*When*—When should the presentation take place?

These are but a few of the questions that should be raised.

The aspects of meeting planning that are most relevant to effective training are developing an agenda, preparing participants for attendance, and checking the facilities. In this chapter, we'll cover these three topics in ample detail to help you avoid the problems that befall the trainer who does not prepare a specific meeting plan.

## WHY MEETINGS FAIL

We have all had the unfortunate experience of attending meetings or training sessions that were largely wasteful of time. What were the reasons a session "bombed"?

When this question was posed to hundreds of experienced trainers around the country, one single answer always surfaced—"lack of preparation!" Without question, poor planning and preparation take their toll far too often.

Other items also play a role in ineffective meetings. These include:

### Lack of a Common Goal

Unless your participants are briefed as to the purpose of the conference or training session, there is no way they can steer toward that end. Your own sights, of course, are set toward an objective; however, if you fail to inform your participants what that objective is, it is very easy for the people in attendance to start down a wrong road and never reach the desired goal. It is up to us to set the ground rules for the meeting and to make sure everyone understands what is expected of them during the session.

### The Wrong People

You have all had the experience of sitting in a meeting and asking yourself, "I wonder why they asked me to come here today?" A common error in many organizations is to issue blanket invitations to people. Very often the people that might be invited to a meeting have no interest, experience, background, or involvement in that conference.

### Poor Scheduling

Even the best communications expert cannot hold the attention of all people at all times. If a meeting does not have a predetermined time length, the participants will tend to sit there and think, "When is this thing going to end?"

### DEVELOPING AN AGENDA

Prior to selection of a site, an agenda should be developed. The agenda establishes the meeting's or training session's requirements. To ensure that your agenda is developed into an effective meeting, use the following guidelines:

1. List the objectives of the meeting.

2. Decide who should attend.

3. Develop criteria for measuring results.

4. Determine the activities that will best achieve the meeting's objectives.

5. Write the content of the program.

### What Are the Objectives of the Meeting?

Like all objectives, the objectives of a meeting must be specific rather than general. The more specific they are, the easier they will be to evaluate. Objectives should be realistic, achievable, measurable, time-related, and ranked in importance, and they should have observable results.

Think carefully about your purpose in developing objectives. Your purpose may be to entertain, educate, change attitudes, change behavior, or solve problems. After deciding which of these broad categories your program falls under, you can then develop more specific objectives.

### Who Should Attend?

Often meetings are called in organizations without regard as to who should or who should not attend. This practice leads to resentment, boredom, and lack of participation. Inviting accountants to a sales training course, for example, might be a waste of their time. They may not be interested, perhaps have no use for the information presented, and would have no way to practice the new skills. Invite only those people who will benefit from your program.

### How Do We Measure Results?

The program results can be measured against the objectives you establish. If the objectives are clear and specific, you will be able to measure them. To test this, make up a few sample questions to check the results. Then attempt to answer the questions and tabulate the answers. If you have trouble in answering the questions, you probably do not have specific objectives. Go back and rewrite the objectives so that they will be measurable.

Now that the objectives have been corrected, prepare the questions and use them for both a pretest and posttest. By giving the same test before and after the meeting, you can measure the change that took place—the learning that occurred during the meeting.

### What Activities Will Best Achieve Those Results?

Developing the activities that achieve the objectives you listed for the meeting is really developing the content of your program. Having zeroed in on specific objectives, you can now develop content and include any game, buzz session, or other activity that will best get the point across to the participants. Techniques to achieve specific training objectives are covered in other chapters.

## MEETING SITE

Many organizations have excellent facilities for their own training sessions. As the field of human resource development receives ever-increasing recognition by these organizations, handsomely equipped training rooms have been added or renovated.

Certainly, if your organization has such facilities, you will likely want to conduct most of your programs on site.

There may be times, however, when you decide to hold a training session at a different location. Perhaps your training responsibilities are such that your classes are held in different cities around the country. How do you pick a site in these cases?

In preparing for an off-site meeting or conference, there are a number of important decisions to be made. While many of these items are relevant to on-site training programs as well, it is doubly important to ensure that all of these factors be considered. In dealing with hotel sales, catering, or convention services departments, you're well advised to look upon these people as part of your team. After all the success of your meeting is important to them also, and they can be of immeasurable help.

### Selecting Meeting Facilities

In selecting a meeting facility, your first concern is to find one that has adequate and comfortable meeting rooms for the number of people you will have at the session. If your group is small, you may find it advantageous to consider a small hotel or motel site.

There are several major questions that you might use as a guide in selecting your meeting site.

- What physical requirements must the facility meet?
- What services must be provided?
- What equipment is necessary?
- Where is the room located?
- How about parking?
- What food service will I need?
- What about costs?
- What is the facility's track record?
- What other concurrent meetings are planned in the hotel?

An on-site inspection gives you an opportunity to visualize the entire program in the actual room(s) it will be conducted in. You can discuss and inform the hotel or convention center personnel of your needs. Problems can often be resolved at this stage that might not be thought of if these premeeting inspections were not made. Misunderstandings about the number of people to attend, the configuration of the class setting, etc., can be cleared up at this time. At this point, you may want to change locations if the hotel can't or won't accommodate you in the way you expect. If everything is satisfactory, get a written agreement at this time spelling out all functions and services to be performed including room rates, complimentary services, etc.

*Write an information letter.* Write a letter to all meeting participants spelling out the details of the meeting. The following checklist may be altered to fit your own needs.

- List the meeting dates, arrival and departure day and time.

- Give the meeting location, hotel or convention center name, and the name of the meeting rooms in the letter.

- Suggested or required dress code.

- Directions by car as well as directions to and from the airport, including courtesy, limo, or cab information.

- The hotel or meeting site phone number.

- Collateral material that may be useful (swim suits, golf clubs, etc.).

- Time and agenda for the meeting.

- Check-out arrangements, including prepaid vs. expense items.

- Breakfast, lunch, dinner, and cocktail arrangements.

- Advance registration procedures, if available.

*Develop a checklist to cover every phase of the meeting.* The following checklists will provide a starting point from which you may develop your own. Pick and choose those items that are relevant and pertinent to your use. You'll find that your tailor-made checklists are an invaluable aid for organizing your meeting.

**What physical requirements must the facility meet?** Generally speaking, nothing can be taken for granted. Many commercial properties, especially the older ones, may not have sufficient electrical outlets, storage space, restrooms in close proximity to the meeting rooms, proper ventilation, or soundproof meeting rooms.

The only way you can be certain that a meeting facility meets your physical requirements is to develop a checklist of your particular requirements and personally visit the site. The following checklist may be helpful and should be altered to fit your needs.

- Size and location of meeting room(s)
- Proximity to additional meeting rooms
- Proximity to restrooms
- Number and location of electrical outlets
- Lighting, switch locations, and dimmer controls
- Ventilation, air-conditioning, and heat controls
- Storage areas
- Wastebaskets
- Transportation
- Union clearances
- Audiovisual equipment

**What services must be provided?** The design of each program, of course, will determine the specific services that will be required. After you have determined the services required for a particular program, you will need to find out who is responsible for that particular activity. The same service may be provided by different service managers in various hotels and motels. To resolve this problem, simply meet with the sales, catering, and food-service managers and find out who is responsible for each of the services you need.

You may wish to develop a checklist of services similar to the one for physical requirements. You might begin the list with:

- Meals
- Menus
- Cocktail parties
- Coffee service
- Message service
- Clean-up services

**What equipment is necessary?** You may have your own equipment and not be concerned with that provided by the off-site property. Often, however, you may find it more convenient to use the facility's equipment than to bring your own. Check first, of course, as to the rental costs and union regulations involved. Many of the newer hotels and convention centers have built-in projectors, screens, tape recorders, and closed-circuit television systems.

A list of equipment will be useful for checking out both the facility's and your own equipment. Items on the following list may be provided partially by the facility and partially from your own stock.

- Projection booth
- Public address system
- Lecterns
- Tables, chairs, and so on
- Display areas
- Projectors and screens
- Easels and chart pads
- Marking pens
- Chalkboards
- Extension cords and adapters

**What is the location?** If your participants are coming from different geographic areas, you will want to check out the accessibility of the selected site. How convenient to freeways, public transportation, or the airport is the location? Is it easy to find for those who may not know the city?

**How about parking?** Don't overlook this all-important item. Is adequate parking space available? Will parking fees be paid by your organization? How handy are loading docks for delivery and pick-up of your training materials?

**What food service will I need?** If you are responsible for meal functions, you will consider the menus and costs for all activities. Don't assume that because a food function is held that the meeting room can be used without cost. The trend is for commercial properties to charge for meeting space even though a catering function is held. Check with the property involved to determine its policy. Another possible catch is in the way costs may be quoted. Some hotels and motels may give you a base price for lunches, coffee breaks, and so on without adding the extra charge for tax and gratuity.

**What is the facility's track record?** In most cases, you are well advised to choose hotels and motels with good reputations for catering to groups such as yours. By checking with experienced trainers in your organization or area, you can quickly find out the past record of a respective site. If you can deal with other professional meeting planners, your own session will be just that much more successful.

**What other events are planned?** When you are finalizing your choice of location, ask the sales department what other groups, if any, will be in the facility when your meeting is scheduled. This is especially important in regard to meeting rooms. Soundproof walls seldom are! Satisfy yourself that the rooms scheduled for your session meet all your criteria.

### Room Arrangements

When dealing with hotel or motel sales or catering personnel, misunderstandings may occur because of terminology. What to one meeting planner may be "schoolroom" setup may mean "theatre style" to someone else. The following terms are generally accepted by professional meeting planners.

*Theater style.* This term is used to describe a room setup in which there are chairs only. As shown in the illustration below, the chairs are typically lined up in straight rows.

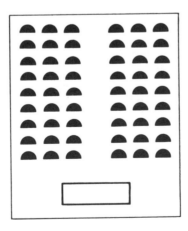

*Classroom style.* This term describes a table-and-chair setup as shown. Ordinarily the furniture is arranged in straight rows. A modified arrangement often affords better eye contact.

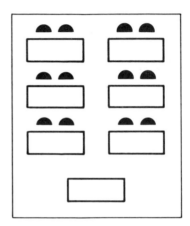

*Conference style.* This may take any of several arrangements. Typically, we use this term to define a table-and-chair setup slightly different from the classroom style. A few variations are as illustrated.

a) U-shape                              b) Conference table

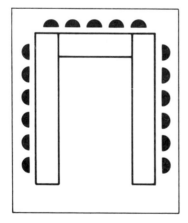                    

c) Closed square

d) Hexagon

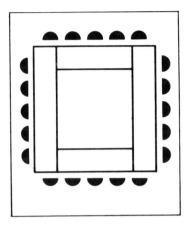

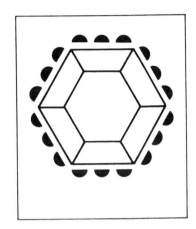

e) Herringbone

f) V-shape

*Banquet style.* In most cases, this refers to a round table setup. Effective for small group discussions, it is not recommended for lecture sessions or where audio or visual aids may present sight or sound problems.

### Suggested Form

Because of the aforementioned confusion with terms, experienced meeting planners will often sketch out their requirements. A sample is shown on the following page. It is a simple worksheet used to serve as a checksheet for times and setups.

**Figure 14-1.** Sample Meeting Planners Form

## Meeting Planners International

Function
Number _____

Meeting
Name <u>1985 PROFESSIONAL</u>　　Date <u>MONDAY, DECEMBER 9, 1985</u>

<u>EDUCATION CONFERENCE</u>　　Time
(start/end) <u>1:30 P.M.–3:00 P.M.</u>

Name of
Function <u>MANAGING CHANGE</u>

Facility <u>POINTE AT TAPATIO CLIFFS</u>　　Room
Name <u>M</u>

Manager/
Budget _____　　Post? <u>YES</u>

Staff
in charge _____　　Guarantee by Date ____ /Time _____

Estim.
Attendance <u>36</u> /Actual _____　　Guarantee ____ /Set ____ /Actual ____

---

**HOTEL/FACILITY TO PROVIDE:**

SETUP: By 12:30 P.M.

· Classroom style for 36 people using 9 (8′ × 18″) tables. (See diagram on next page, Function # _____.)

· Ice water, and glassware on each table.

· Ashtrays on one side of room only.

· Handouts table (8′ × 18″) at entrance to room, skirted.

· Easel outside door for sign.

· (1) chair for ticket-taker outside door.

· (1) (8′ × 30″) speaker's table.

· (1) chair for speaker's table.

· Ice water, glassware on speaker's table.

· Table lectern.

A/V REQUIREMENTS:

(1) 16 mm movie projector
(1) screen
(1) overhead
(1) flipchart and pad with marker

**OTHERS TO PROVIDE:**

SPEAKER(S):

Edward E. Scannell

MPI TO PROVIDE:

Meeting Room Sign _____
Lectern Cover _____
Speaker's Sign _____
Smoking Sign _____
Recording Card _____
Handouts _____

MEETING ROOM CHAIRMAN:

Speaker Introduction _____
Evaluations _____
Attendance Count _____
Speaker's Certificate _____
Speaker's Gift _____

# CHAPTER 15

# Conducting a Meeting

*Lights . . . camera . . . action!*

Much as on the Hollywood sound set, your efforts during the days and weeks or months of planning all peak on "opening day." Whether it's really your first day or your fiftieth year in the training business, you should realize that all those nervous "first-day" feelings are not only commonplace, but even welcomed! Senior trainers are of the firm opinion that these nervous tensions make us even more anxious to overcome them and do a better job.

This chapter will offer you some tested and workable ideas that you will find helpful in conducting meetings. You will learn several methods to acclimate a new group to the training process. You will find that by using these "warm-up exercises," you are also putting yourself more at ease with your trainees and therefore establishing an atmosphere truly conducive to learning.

This chapter also covers all aspects of leading or conducting a meeting or conference. Whether your training session is composed of only two or three individuals, or two or three hundred, you will find useful techniques in this chapter that will make your meeting successful.

## OPENING ACTIVITIES

The initial activities used to open a meeting set the flavor for the entire session. If the opening is interesting and purposeful, and if it relates to the needs of the participants, then you will capture their interest. They will then be attentive and probably participate in the meeting activities.

Remember those first-day jitters? Don't forget that your new trainees have the same fears and anxieties you have!

In questioning participants attending actual sessions in which the people did not know each other, the authors have found these types of unasked questions:

"What kind of a teacher are we going to have?"

"How come my boss told me I had to come?"

"Are they going to give tests?"

"Who else is going to be here?"

"Do I have as good a background as the rest of these people?"

These are but a few of the questions and concerns people have. Remember that for some people "going back to school"—that is, your training session—is a serious, traumatic experience. Perhaps their own formal schooling was less than adequate. Perhaps they have a deep psychological fear of not being able to learn. Your task is keenly important. You must dispel those fears and establish a friendly climate.

### Breaking the Ice

There are several ways you can help set a foundation of informality, which is so often a prerequisite to learning. As discussed in Chapter 10, the law of effect suggests that people learn best in a friendly setting. To assist you in building that atmosphere, here are some proven ways to help new participants (and yourself!) get things started.

*Self-introductions.* This is by far the most commonly used technique. Simply stated, each person introduces himself or herself and gives a brief background sketch. Keep it light and informal.

*Mutual introductions.* As a refreshing variation of the typical self-introduction, this method has each person introduce someone else. For example, in a group of twenty-four people, have them count off one to twelve (or to half of whatever group size is involved). The thirteenth person restarts the sequence as number one; the fourteenth, number two; and so on. Then ask each half of each paired number (number one meets number one, number twelve meets number twelve, and so on) to find his or her counterpart across the room. Allow them five to eight minutes to give each other enough background information so they can be introduced by the *other* person to the entire group. After they all return to their original seats, start the introductions.

*Circle introductions.* If your training is set in a U-shape or some other circular or horseshoe fashion where everyone can physically see the entire group, try this:

You as the trainer start the process by saying, "My name is (Pat)." The first person at your front left says, "My name is (Joe)" then repeats your name and restates his own, in other words, (Pat, Joe). The person to Joe's left repeats the process adding her name, "My name is Jane— Pat, Joe, Jane" and so on until the entire group is completed.

As you introduce this game, you will have to reassure your participants they can actually accomplish this feat. They will have grave reservations until they prove to themselves it actually works. The authors have used this technique with groups as large as 75 to 100. As long as people can see each other, it can work.

It is also an excellent illustration of the law of repetition, that is, performing a task over and over and over again.

*Name cards.* Table tent cards showing the name, department, and so on, of the participant are always helpful in assisting us to learn each other's names. Make sure the names are large enough to be seen and are written on *both* sides of the tent card so fellow participants can also see the name.

*Humor.* An opening story or two, given in good taste and relating to something about the topic, is usually well received. If you don't feel comfortable with this, however, don't do it!

### Climate Setting

In a training session, you can establish a favorable learning climate by subtly suggesting that the session will be informal. Your actions, as conference leader, indicate to the participants the kind of climate they can expect. If you act relaxed and friendly, smile, and open the meeting in a warm and informal way, your participants will feel comfortable and be more relaxed and willing to participate.

The following techniques will help establish a favorable climate:

- Specify the benefits and objectives that the participants will derive from attending the meeting. If the benefits appeal to the participants, they will be more willing to share the responsibility for learning the material presented.

- Speak to the participants as peers rather than as students or subordinates. Give them a feeling of "We're doing this together" by using "we" and "our" rather than "you" and "your."

- Treat mistakes as steps in the learning process. When mistakes are treated as a natural occurrence, the participants get a feeling of freedom. They feel free to try new activities without fear of criticism. Trust is also developed in an atmosphere that provides the proper climate for change.

- Relate part of the new material to the past experiences of the partici-

**151**

pants. Also use words and examples that are familiar to them—words that are part of their job vocabulary.

- Provide an easy task related to the meeting objectives so the participants can experience early success. Research has shown that early success creates a more comfortable feeling and motivates participants to try to learn more.

You can develop other climate-setting techniques to add to the preceding list. Just think of good practices that you have observed when attending a meeting and incorporate those into your plan.

## INTEREST-BUILDING TECHNIQUES

Even when your opening activities are outstanding, they will not necessarily guarantee that you will retain your participants' attention and interest throughout the meeting. Climate building must continue throughout the meeting. The following are only a few of the techniques that will build and retain interest.

### Some Meeting Guides

The following climate-building techniques are especially useful in training or problem-solving meetings. These techniques have been tested and used successfully in numerous meetings.

- Clearly state the objectives of the meeting and the benefits the participants will receive.

- Provide an opportunity for group discussion.

- Design participation into the meeting by posing problems for class solution.

- Provide achievement-oriented activities.

- Relate all examples and anecdotes to the training situation and to the background of the participants.

- Try to determine and relate to the skill level of each participant.

- Permit some class input in determining what part of your presentation to concentrate on.

### Testing the Agenda: A Seven-Point Guide

You can develop interest and at the same time determine what parts of the meeting require more emphasis and what parts should be downgraded. By testing the agenda, you see firsthand the items the participants are concerned with and those they find boring or of little value. The following points, if recorded and utilized, will enable you to react to participant interest and improve your meeting.

- List the major meeting topics on a flipchart.

- Get agreement from the group on the ground rules.

- Ask for comments, opinions, ideas, and feelings about each of the topics listed on the flipchart.

- Ask "let's suppose" or "in your experience" questions to draw out all members of the group.

- If one topic is seriously criticized, ask for other opinions. Remember, disagreement can be used to trigger further discussion.

- Summarize frequently what the group has said.

- Record responses on a note pad to use as a guide in conducting the meeting.

### Small Group Discussion Sessions

Small groups become affable and provide members with a method of fulfilling their social and esteem needs. Small groups have a motivating influence on the individual group members. Members develop an elite feeling about membership in the group. Because of the synergy (the whole being greater than the sum of its parts) developed in group interactions, and the positive support the group gives the members, members may feel that they are more productive than other groups. This feeling motivates more interest, attention, and harder work. It's easy to see why such groups become more productive.

The obvious generalization for training is that learning can be enhanced by small discussion groups. In a small group, the members can discuss and digest information in a neutral environment. They are free to examine and test ideas without the pressure of old habits that have formed under specific work conditions affecting their evaluations of the new techniques.

### Resolving Disagreements

Some disagreement will occur in every meeting, even if the meeting involves only two people. It is utterly impossible for everyone to agree on every point that is covered in a meeting. Different perceptions, based upon each individual's unique experiences, lead to confusion, misinterpretation, and, of course, disagreement. Disagreement cannot be avoided, but it can be confronted and managed.

- Use disagreement to stimulate group discussion.

- Explore each side in depth and watch for possible applications for each view.

- Expand the discussion to subjects that take on more importance than the original question to gain collaboration from the group.

- Look for segments within each argument that both sides can agree upon, thus lessening the area of disagreement.

- Summarize and clarify the points made by both sides.

- Let the group decide the issue.

- If agreement can't be reached, state the problem as being unresolved and move to the next topic.

## HOW TO LEAD A CONFERENCE

A simplified and workable approach to leading conferences can be modified from the four-step method discussed in Chapter 10. These four steps—preparation, presentation, discussion, and summarization—are the same four that should be followed when you are ready to make your plans for leading a group meeting.

### Preparation

In planning for any type of a conference, the first question that must be seriously answered is "Do you really *need* a conference? Why?"

While this may seem like a rather basic question, it is all too often taken for granted; for example, "We always meet on Tuesday mornings," or "But we always meet to discuss these items," or "When Mr. Smith was here, we always. . . ." In other words, because we've always held a conference for staff meetings, training sessions, or a host of other items is simply *not* a good enough answer as to why this meeting should be held.

Assuming, however, that the first question *is* satisfactorily answered, then the four-step method will fall neatly into place. In planning and preparing for the group meeting, it goes without saying that you as the trainer or conference leader will have first determined the need and set forth the objective of the particular session. If the group is not aware of the time limitations for this particular conference, those, too, should be explained.

In putting the group at ease, the new trainer has a real advantage over a senior counterpart. Since the new trainer is likely to feel a bit ill at ease, then it stands to reason that the new trainees or conference attendees will be coming from that same mold. By putting the group at ease with a cordial greeting and a sincere and warm welcome to the meeting, the trainer sets the stage for the air of informality. As mentioned earlier, an appropriate anecdote or story may break the ice and help create the right atmosphere, but the trainer is again cautioned to make certain the point or punch line of the story is relevant to the item or situation being discussed. Other introductory comments on the part of the trainer would include setting up the ground rules and defining the overall procedural plan for that particular meeting.

It is also imperative that the trainer or discussion leader redefine the purposes for that meeting or the goals or objectives for that training session. While this may seem like a very basic point, it is so often forgotten that the question is often asked by the attendee, "Why am I here, I wonder if I am really in the right meeting?"

In short, we are really talking about a total preparation of yourself as the conference leader, the room, the equipment (visual aids and so on), your training materials, your lesson plan, and a multitude of items that will help make this session effective.

### Presentation

After setting forth the ground rules and preparing the group and yourself for the meeting, it is wise to move right into the topic of the conference. Experienced conference leaders attest to the fact that it is very common to experience difficulty in eliciting the first comment from the participants, but once that first comment is offered, there seems to be a free and full flow of ideas and comments back and forth across the room. Let us discuss a simple method that will help you in your goal of starting the discussion off in a proper way. If you use this method, these simple steps should be followed in sequence:

1. *Broad introduction.* By giving a broad introductory statement of the conference or problem to be discussed, the trainer or conference leader purposely tries to draw a general picture of the topic that is on the table. It is easy to see, of course, that the bigger the picture, the more likely the participants will feel a part *of*—as opposed to apart *from*—the problem. Therefore, it is important that the introductory statement be very broad and encompassing in nature.

2. *Delimitation.* The next step is for you to acknowledge that while the broad statement outlined in step 1 is of real import, there is simply not the time to discuss all the ramifications of that major issue. Therefore, the second step is to delimit the problem into manageable portions for your conference.

3. *Information.* To ascertain that all of the participants are coming from the same background and have the same general bits of information,

the trainer is well advised to give specific information concerning the problems or issues for the meeting. For example, if the session is for the purpose of discussing ways of reducing absenteeism in a particular department, the first step (broad statement) would be to identify the problem and perhaps give some general facts and figures illustrating the severity of absenteeism in the industry or organization. The second step then follows, of course, to pinpoint the information and to narrow down the problem as it affects our particular division, department, or agency. Here, then, in our third step, we would relate specific bits of information as they pertain only in and solely to our particular group. Another advantage of giving specific information is that it overcomes the common problem of assuming that everybody knows what we are talking about. This way we can ensure that all of the conferees have the same background and information.

In following the previous three steps and narrowing down the problem, the way we phrase the initial question is of extreme importance. Obviously a simple question that can be answered with a "yes" or a "no" is usually not a sufficiently important problem on which to have a conference. But attitudinal types of questions can be phrased to really draw out the participants. For example, questions that begin with a "what, why, when, how, or where" usually succeed in getting a good discussion going.

While this basic method has been field tested and is acknowledged as being workable, we are not trying to say that it is a guaranteed way to get participants quickly involved in the discussion. The art of questioning is a tool that the new trainer must learn. For our purposes in this section, two basic types of questions will be illustrated:

1. *The overhead question.* The overhead question is essentially one that is thrown out to the entire group for discussion. It is a shotgun type of inquiry that is really directed at no one in particular. For example, "How might we be able to lessen absenteeism in our department?" followed momentarily by a pause is an overhead question.

2. *The direct question.* The second type of question, the direct question, implies that the inquiry is targeted at a specific individual. For example, "Bill, how do you think we might lessen absenteeism in our department?" directs that question to one respondent.

While there are pros and cons to both sides of the coin, in most cases the overhead question is preferred. Better yet would be a combination of the two. As an example, ask the question "How might we lessen absenteeism in our department?", wait a few seconds, and then ask, "Bill, what are your ideas?" With this method all of the participants are hopefully going to pay attention to the question since they know they might be asked for a response.

Since we are throwing a question out to the entire group, we are really demanding the attention of all. The direct question, by its very nature, may let the rest of the group "off the hook" after the trainer calls on someone for a response.

Another way to start discussion is for the trainer to give his or her own opinion on the topic at the outset of the program. You are cautioned, however, on the possible controversy this may cause. While in most cases this is not a recommended tactic, there are times when a planted item such as this—which you know will stir controversy—will really get discussion going in a hurry. Use this technique with caution and only if you are fully aware of its impact.

## Discussion

At this point, after the sequential planning and presentation, the discussion is ready to go full speed ahead. By definition, a conference is an exchange of ideas. And the conference *leader* is exactly that. In other words, she or he is not a lecturer but rather a facilitator for a group discussion. It is, therefore, the function of conference leaders to encourage participation in a free and full flow of comments, ideas, and attitudes. It is important, too, for them to readily acknowledge that they *do not* have all the answers. They should encourage the group to pool their ideas and exchange their experiences so that all can benefit from the various backgrounds and experiences.

While discussion is an instructive tool, we should also look at some problem areas of how to control discussion. Occasionally, we will run into a type of personality, such as a talkative person, who tends to monopolize the conversation. In this case, it is very important for the conference leader to talk tactfully to that person during a break period to point out that he or she is monopolizing the conversation and preventing others from being heard. Sometimes a form of group pressure will perform that task for the discussion leader.

Keeping the discussion on target is perhaps one of the most difficult chores of the trainer. In conferences, we must always realize what our goal is for that particular meeting. If we find we are straying somewhat from the topic at hand, we as discussion leaders must quickly bring the group back whenever necessary. Certainly there are times when side discussions might be encouraged, but more often than not we tend to get too far off base and run off on dozens of tangents that are really not pertinent to the meeting.

## Summarization

Experienced conference leaders recognize the need to summarize and recap the comments of their group at frequent intervals. By pointing out some of the highlights and major points discussed, the entire group will review the progress of the discussion. So many times we attend a meeting and leave that meeting wondering "what next?" Unfortunately, many times we never seem to find out the results of our discussions. For this reason, the discussion leader must indicate what follow through, if any, will be taken. If the group has reached the end of the discussion and has pretty much attained the goal of that conference, of course, it is time to stop. The group should decide on a follow-through plan of action and then should be advised at a later date what happened after the meeting in the way of any additional action taken by others in the company.

## SUMMARY

This section has attempted to offer you several field-tested ideas and practices that you can use tomorrow. The guides and procedures outlined herein have been proven effective in hundreds of training programs across the country. Whether you're a novice teacher or a senior trainer, these methods, if used properly, will work for you.

# CHAPTER 16

# Problem Participants

*Where'd I lose control?*

There comes a time in every trainer's life when something goes wrong! Sometimes these things are beyond the trainer's control—most times, they are not.

This chapter will introduce several potential problem areas or pesky personalities that may surface on occasion.

Let's agree at the start that by far the majority of people in your session will be positive, friendly, and supportive of your efforts. But it would be naive to suggest that this is always the case. Let's prepare for those rare situations so you'll know how to handle them if they ever come up.

We'll start by looking at a few situations that may arise during a training session, then we'll discuss some types of distracting or "people-problem" areas.

## HANDLING PROBLEMS

### Speeding Up the Session

This common problem occurs in a number of training meetings. Maybe the people just can't seem to get fired up about the problem under discussion. If you find silent faces, you might call on individuals by name for their responses. You occasionally may even want to misstate a reply on the part of a respondent, which should bring additional comments from others in the room. Many times your frank comment that things are moving too slowly will spark some of the people to get the session back on the beam. If a comment provokes a quizzical stare or shaking of a head in disagreement, call on that person to ask how he/she feels about the comment. You can also use debatable questions to get things moving. Finally, if your items are moving along too slowly, merely move to another point.

## Slowing Down the Session

You've done so well with the first problem of speeding things up that now things may be going too quickly. Occasionally you may have a group that is quite excited about the topic and the ideas are coming too fast to synthesize and summarize properly. Should this be the case, your job is to slow down the program by asking certain respondents to clarify their comments and amplify some of them. You will also summarize more frequently and occasionally write some of the items on the chalkboard or flipchart you are using in the room. You can usually tell from some of the looks around the room if participants are being hurried to cover too many topics in full measure. If this is the case, merely stop and ask for full discussion on some of the points already discussed.

## Sidetracking of Problems

Another common problem is that your participants may tend to get off on side issues that have no relevance to the main problem. If this is the case, quickly restate the problem or write it on the board to make sure all are back in tune with you. You might also want to ask someone how the item or comment might apply to the problem being discussed. Listen attentively because you may find that what to you is a side issue is very much a part of the item under discussion. If you find you can tell a quick or humorous anecdote about the side issue, it is then easy to restart the conference after the people have had a quick laugh. As mentioned earlier, there are times when you may want to sidetrack the conference if the topic or time is in your favor.

## People Problems

At some time, you might encounter a difficult "people problem." Some people may exhibit a negative behavior pattern that could interfere with learning and cause difficulty for the trainer and the rest of the group. The professional trainer must learn to deal with these disruptive matters in a way that wins the respect of the group.

Keep in mind that it may not be necessary to intervene each time a participant disrupts the class with seemingly inappropriate behavior. Some negative behavior may not be worthy of intervention and often other participants will assist and correct the unruly individual. You, as the instructor, should intervene when the disruptive behavior becomes repetitive or is having a negative impact on the group.

There are a number of roles that participants may play, depending upon their own ego needs and psychological background. Since these behaviors are ego-related, we need to deal with them in a way that preserves the ego, if possible. The points suggested for the disruptive roles listed are designed to respect the individual where possible, but also to handle the situation using a win–win method.

*The know-it-all.* This type of individual is the self-styled expert on any and all questions. He or she seemingly has an opinion about everything and may confront, correct, or even contradict what you say.

First, and most important, don't respond in kind; that is, don't embarrass the person or be sarcastic. Oddly enough, this person can often be a strong ally and supporter, so don't make him or her look bad.

Often the group will handle this type of behavior by nonverbal or verbal responses. Your position can be to "disagree agreeably." If this negative behavior continues, the group typically becomes more vocal for you.

If the debate continues, privately and tactfully suggest that the offender give others a chance to participate. You can assign this person the role of recorder, keeping him or her too busy writing to talk.

*The talkative individual.* Closely aligned but far less negative, you may find one or two people who tend to be extremely vocal on any issue or point raised. They may or may not be talking from experience, but one thing is certain—they are talking! While we have stressed the importance of getting all people to take part in your session, you cannot let one or two monopolize the entire conversation. Therefore, in order to be fair to the rest of the people in your program, you must deal firmly but fairly with this type of individual. If they insist on "blowing steam," make them give reasons for their thinking. Consistently ask them to back up their opinions or comments. Instead of your commenting on their remarks, again direct them to the rest of the group and ask for the group's opinions on what is being said. While we are treating "talkers" as a problem area, it is well to recognize that they, too, may be the people who can really make the conference an excellent one. We are concerned here only with the people who tend to overplay their hand and do not give others the chance for full participation.

*The silent person.* Just as you might have vocal and argumentative people in your session, you might also encounter the person who never says anything. Perhaps he or she is bored, indifferent, or even insecure. This is a silent type who sincerely needs your assistance at the meeting. Seat these people in the front of the room so that they can be close to you. You will be able to see their faces and, when you see a twinkle in their eyes, call for a comment. People who are sensitive or silent may simply need reassurance. They may be fearful of the rest of the group or afraid that their comments or ideas may be laughed at by the other conferees. Give them all the moral support you can, even if they stumble and make a comment that seems to be irrelevant to the discussion. Quickly thank them for their comments and add, "In other words, Jim, you are saying . . ." and then make the comment that is as nearly pertinent as you possibly can. Your function as trainer is not to embarrass anybody. This person can become your most fervent friend by being properly handled during your program. Be careful also not to seat a silent type alongside the argumentative or talkative type. Too often the verbal person will squelch any possible comments that might have been forthcoming from the sensitive individual. The silent person is indeed worthy of your attention. Ask easier questions, and then when a quiet person answers, a word of praise will uplift his or her morale and self-confidence.

*The griper.* The griper continually finds fault with all aspects of the program. He or she may be dissatisfied with the classroom, the location, the materials being used, the equipment, the methods, or the content of the course. Be prepared for comments like, "I hate role play," "This equipment doesn't work very well," etc.

Try to determine the basis of the complaints. Check out the possibility of one vocal comment really representing the opinion of several others who feel the same way but did not say so. Obviously, if the complaints are justified, take prompt, corrective action.

If their criticism concerns a policy or item that cannot be changed, point this out. Sometimes, a minor change or adaptation may rectify the situation. Let the complainer suggest a solution and have the group react. Channel the negative into a positive whenever possible. If all else fails, privately discuss the problem with the individual. As a last resort, let the person withdraw from the program if the behavior is disruptive.

*The rescuer.* The rescuer means well and is motivated to protect others. By finding excuses for others who make mistakes, he/she is attempting to excuse mistakes in general. The rescuer apologizes, defends, explains, and interprets for others when those others have been corrected or when they are obviously wrong.

The rescuer will say things like, "What Joe was trying to say was . . ." or "I think what Sally meant was . . ." The appropriate intervention for the instructor is to say, "I know you are speaking for Joe but, to avoid misunderstanding, let's let Joe speak for himself," or you might say, "I know you mean well, but it would be more helpful to Sally if we let her clarify her own thoughts."

*The wanderer.* This individual continually seems to ramble farther and farther away from the question being discussed. Glance at your watch, politely interrupt, thank the person for the thought, but suggest that time is short and the group must return to the main issue. Don't let the wanderer carry on too long or you may lose the entire group. Be courteous but firm.

*Clashing personalities.* If you find a couple of participants engaged in heated discussions, you'll need to play the role of a referee. Handle this quickly. Don't allow tempers to flare. Suggest that each opinion may be correct or emphasize the points of agreement. Acknowledge that opposing viewpoints are healthy and can even be constructive, but divorce the comment from the individual. Don't criticize either individual.

If conflicts persist, call a break and talk to the participants directly, asking that disagreements be omitted.

## SUMMARY

It is important to restate our opening premise that most groups are great to work with and are usually supportive and appreciative of your efforts. Remember, even in those rare cases of confrontation or dissension, the majority will be on your side. Maintain control and never lose your cool!

# CHAPTER 17

# Evaluation

*You dun good.*

Few things in the field of human resource development create as much controversy or discussion as does the word *evaluation*. Serious trainers will always agree on the need for critical appraisal and improvement; we seldom, however, agree on the best method of evaluation.

This chapter will discuss the process of evaluation and offer several field-tested models and techniques for such review.

A basic premise underlying our entire approach to evaluation is that it is a continuing process. We must always be asking our peers and ourselves: "How can I make my next session even better?" If we indeed believe that education is a continuing process, it would seem to follow that we should always be learning and benefiting from our own mistakes of omission and commission.

## WHY EVALUATE?

Let's first ask why we need to evaluate in the first place. These few responses will answer that inquiry:

*Mandate.* If your organization, like most, requires some type of evaluative response to training from participants and instructors, that's not a bad reason in itself; in other words, "My boss told me I had to!"

*Improvement.* We should always strive to make tomorrow's sessions better than today's. Certainly we want to continue to improve our own performance, and participants' and colleagues' critiques can be used constructively to aid us in that effort.

*Justification.* There are many times when we are called upon to defend or justify the continuation of a certain class or program. If we can produce objective data that honestly serve that purpose, a reviewer is able to quickly recognize the real worth and value of the program to the organization.

As mentioned previously, experienced trainers are quick to attack or defend a particular form of evaluation. Many training directors feel that appraisals done by participants at the conclusion of a program offer little more than a "happiness rating." Appraisal forms, some trainers suggest, provide little more than a "halo effect." Perhaps this is true, but experience indicates that, while some trainees may tell you only what you want to hear, most participants, if given the protection of anonymity, will be honest and fair in their critique.

Trainers are likely to be the most critical audience in the world—as well they should be! Trainers and trainees have the right to expect the best, and most trainers are ready to point out when these expectations aren't met.

## ELEMENTS OF EVALUATION

In brief, evaluation can be seen as having four components. To be complete and thorough, your plan should have provisions for all four segments. With the pressures of time, money, and effort, however, we often will use only one of the key parts. While this approach can be acknowledged as better than no evaluation at all, it must be remembered that our findings are never totally complete unless provision is made also to check out the other segments.

Dr. Don Kirkpatrick of the University of Wisconsin is making a continuing study of the evaluation areas for human resource development. He suggests that the four main areas of evaluation are:

1. *Reaction.* What did the participants say about the program?

2. *Learning.* What knowledge, skills, or attitudes were learned?

3. *Behavior.* As defined, learning is a change in behavior. Did the training actually bring forth a change in behavior?

4. *Results.* This could be the most important—the bottom line. Did our training pay off? Did it really do what it was supposed to do?

### Instruments for Evaluation

There are numerous devices for collecting and measuring training effectiveness. You may have to design one for the specific purpose of evaluating the training program you conduct. The techniques listed here are commonly used:

| *Instrument* | *Measures* |
|---|---|
| • Pretests and posttests | • Learning |
| • Observation | • Change in behavior |

**165**

- Work reports
- Questionnaires

- Interviews

- Management ratings

- Results on the job
- Trainees' perception of training or change
- Interviewer's perception of change
- Management's perception of change

## EFFECTIVE EVALUATION

As indicated earlier, we believe that, to be effective and useful, evaluation must cover every element in the program—beginning with program design and continuing through to on-the-job performance results. This can be accomplished by evaluating key elements:

- The program

- The presenter

- The trainees

- On-the-job results

## THE PROCESS OF EVALUATION

If your program is designed with thought given to the evaluation process, evaluation can be an easier task. Many trainers use an evaluation form as a guide in designing a lesson or presentation. By so doing, they can anticipate and avoid future problems. The basic process of evaluation is to collect data related to the program's objectives and tabulate and analyze these data.

### Data Collection

There are four basic data collection techniques that are useful to trainers. They are the questionnaire, interview, tests, and observation. We will not explore these in detail as there are many excellent books available on this subject. Our intent is to provide merely a brief overview of the value of each technique.

*Questionnaires* are the most popular instrument used by trainers. They are easily administered but are deceivingly simple. Care must be taken to give the participants a range of responses wide enough to express their true feelings. A wide variety of questions is necessary to ensure validity. The value of questionnaires is that you can collect data on the feelings, opinions, thoughts, and beliefs of the respondents. People are often reluctant to express their views openly in a group, but will do so quite willingly in writing, especially if they can do so anonymously.

*Interviews* are useful to gather in-depth information and reduce some of the bias in questionnaires. If an answer indicates that the respondent doesn't understand the question, the interviewer can clarify that item. The value of interviewing is its flexibility. The interviewer can alter the kind of questioning to respond to the concerns of the respondent. If the respondent introduces a new relevant topic, the interviewer can explore it.

*Tests* are valuable in determining how much the student has learned. Tests in program evaluation should be designed to test comprehension. Devise the test so that each segment of the program can be evaluated individually. Then, individual segments can be rewritten to improve clarity.

*Observation,* one of the most valuable techniques an instructor has, is often the least used. Students are reacting to a session either nonverbally or verbally all the time. Instructors or presenters who watch the facial expressions and other body movements of their trainees get immediate and valuable feedback. If you see blank stares or puzzled looks, you'll know you're not getting through. You can then correct by asking for questions or open discussion. The value of using observation for evaluation is that you can immediately alter your presentation to fit class needs.

## Analysis and Revision

Once the data have been collected, you must tabulate the results and determine their significance. This may require a minimal or a great amount of time, depending upon the number of the respondents and the number of questions asked.

The answers may be statistically analyzed or merely interpreted on the basis of the larger number of answers being most significant. In analyzing data, look for causes. Wherever possible, identify specific problems that can be corrected by revising the program.

When making a program revision, look at the individual essay responses. Often one comment will relate to a program weakness that does not show up in the statistics. The only way to do this, of course, is to look at the raw data. When all data have been reviewed, then make the necessary program revisions.

In summary, the evaluative process is one of comparing results against objectives. The difficulty comes in determining what the results are. The process of evaluation has been reduced to the following steps:

1. Collect the data.

2. Arrange and analyze the data.

3. Interpret and draw conclusions from the data.

4. Compare the conclusions to the stated objectives.

5. Record recommendations for changes in the next program.

## EVALUATING THE PROGRAM

Our primary question in evaluating the program should be "Was the purpose of the training program accomplished?" To answer this question, we must look at the program objectives. We then measure the program design in relation to those objectives. Next we measure the value of the program content, and, finally, the usefulness of the content, always relating to the stated objectives of the program.

### Checking the Program Design Against Objectives

Lay out the specific objectives that were stated at the beginning of the program. Now pick out specific portions of the training program and list the elements of the program that will train the student to achieve that object. Continue this process until all the key elements have been shown to serve a specific function in reaching the stated objectives.

If you have program elements that don't fit one of the objectives, then your evaluation must identify that element as not relating to the objectives. If, on the other hand, you have an objective with nothing listed under it, you must report the design as being deficient in providing for that objective. If the objective was reached due to some other activity, indicate so in your report so that it may be incorporated as a planned activity.

The following checklist provides a general guide for design evaluation:

- Were the program objectives stated in clear, specific terms?

- Were the objectives measurable, realistically attainable, and performance oriented?

- Was the design flexible enough to be adapted to different student needs and abilities?

- Did the design embody adult training methods?

- Did the design incorporate a method of testing the students to determine what they learned?

- Will what the student learned satisfy job requirements and management expectations?

- Did the design reasonably fit the money budgeted for the program?

**Measuring the Value of the Program Content**

The value of program content can be determined by examining students' reactions. If the students participate by making comments and asking questions, and show a general interest in an activity, the activity has value. If, on the other hand, the students sit quietly, act bored, and pay little attention, then the content likely has very little value to them. To have value the content should evoke interest and participation from the students.

**Measuring the Usefulness of the Program Content**

The usefulness of the program content can be determined by relating it to specific functions the trainee must perform. The question is "Will the content of this program be useful to the trainee in performing the job?" This information can be acquired by comparing the performance aspects of the training with individual job descriptions or by questioning the trainee.

Throughout the program, you should continually check for usefulness. Ask the trainee questions such as, "How will you be able to apply this on the job?"; "Which of these principles can you apply?"; and "What problems do you see in applying these ideas at work?" These same questions can be included in a questionnaire and given at the end of the program. Even if you have asked them orally, repeat them on the questionnaire to include those participants who do not normally respond orally.

## EVALUATING THE PRESENTERS

Experienced instructors welcome the feedback that comes from evaluation. They recognize the opportunity for growth that evaluation provides. As a new trainer, however, you may feel defensive when being evaluated. You may feel especially defensive when the evaluation is in writing, where it seems to be a permanent criticism. You will lose this feeling and welcome evaluation once you realize it is meant to be helpful rather than critical and that it may be a reliable source of growth-producing information for you.

**Using the Trainees as Evaluators**

You can never tell with complete accuracy how you come across to your participants—but they can and will tell you. The questionnaire, of course, is the most popular instrument for this purpose. Trainees are not professional trainers, however, and should not be expected to evaluate highly technical aspects of the presenter's performance. Questions for trainees should be tailored to personal reactions, feelings, and general observations. The following list covers areas that the trainee may appropriately be asked to evaluate.

- Did the instructor hold your interest?
- Did the explanations sufficiently answer your questions?
- Did you understand the instructor's objectives?
- What part of the presentation did you like best?
- What part of the presentation did you like least?
- Was the instructor's language clear or confusing?
- How did the instructor help you?
- Was your learning affected by the instructor's personality and manner?
- How well do you think the instructor knew the subject?
- How well was the instructor prepared?
- How appropriate was the instructor's rate of presentation (fast, slow)?
- Were the instructor's summaries clear?

Following are several sample forms of actual evaluations used in training programs.

# SESSION EVALUATION

| SESSION # | SPEAKER(S) | | MY GROUP ROLE IS: |
|-----------|-----------|---|---|
| MY EXPERIENCE LEVEL IS: | NEW | EXPERIENCED | VERY EXPERIENCED |

**LEARNING OUTCOME**

not at all                                                                totally

- The announced objectives were met:

| 0 | 1 | 2 | 3 | 4 | 5 |

- This session helped me to meet my
  personal conference goals:

not at all                                                                totally

**OVERALL SESSION RATING**

poor                                                                     superior

- Content delivery was:

| 0 | 1 | 2 | 3 | 4 | 5 |

- Speakers delivery was:

poor                                                                     superior

What specific feedback do you have about this session?  To:  Speaker ☐   ASTD Staff ☐   Conference Committee ☐

Please place completed evaluation forms in the collection boxes provided in most session rooms.

**REACTION SHEET**

Subject _____  Date _____

Speaker/Leader _____

   Your reactions and comments will help us determine whether our programs meet your needs and interests. They will also provide a basis for program improvement.

1. Reaction to **Subject**
   - ☐ Excellent                    Comments:
   - ☐ Very Good
   - ☐ Good
   - ☐ Fair
   - ☐ Poor

2. Reaction to **Speaker/Leader**  (if more than one, insert name next to rating)
   - ☐ Excellent                    Comments:
   - ☐ Very Good
   - ☐ Good
   - ☐ Fair
   - ☐ Poor

3. What did you find most valuable?




4. Suggested improvements?

**MPI Professional Education Conference**
# COURSE EVALUATION FORM

DATE: _____

COURSE TITLE: _____

COURSE SPEAKER: _____

*Please rate the course and speaker on the following items: (circle one numer)*

| | LOW | | | | | | HIGH |
|---|---|---|---|---|---|---|---|
| Knowledge of Subject | 1 | 2 | 3 | 4 | 5 | 6 | 7 |
| Ability to Present Ideas Clearly | 1 | 2 | 3 | 4 | 5 | 6 | 7 |
| Ability to Adapt to Audience Needs | 1 | 2 | 3 | 4 | 5 | 6 | 7 |
| Ability to Provide Usable Ideas | 1 | 2 | 3 | 4 | 5 | 6 | 7 |
| Ability to Utilize Audiovisuals | 1 | 2 | 3 | 4 | 5 | 6 | 7 |
| Ability to Actively Involve Audience | 1 | 2 | 3 | 4 | 5 | 6 | 7 |
| Ability to Use Humor | 1 | 2 | 3 | 4 | 5 | 6 | 7 |
| Ability to Handle Questions from Audience | 1 | 2 | 3 | 4 | 5 | 6 | 7 |
| Ability to Pace Speed of Delivery | 1 | 2 | 3 | 4 | 5 | 6 | 7 |
| Ability to Choose Proper Vocabulary or Level | 1 | 2 | 3 | 4 | 5 | 6 | 7 |
| Overall Appearance | 1 | 2 | 3 | 4 | 5 | 6 | 7 |
| Confidence as Speaker/Trainer | 1 | 2 | 3 | 4 | 5 | 6 | 7 |

Was the presentation relevant to your job? _____
_____

Was the content what you expected from reading the program? _____
_____

Would you ask the speaker to present again? _____
_____

What could be done to improve the course? _____
_____

Other comments? _____
_____

*(Please complete and return your evaluation at the conclusion of the course. Thank you.)*

# 1984 ASTD CONFERENCE EVALUATION

Your cooperation in completing this session evaluation will enable future National Conference Program Design Committees to continue ASTD's commitment to the highest quality, most beneficial and productive Conference speakers and sessions.

Session # _____    Registration # _____

Speaker _____

**ATTENDEE INFORMATION**   Place an X or fill in box as appropriate.

I. Level of Experience (in years)

| | 1 | 2 | 3-5 | 10 or more |
|---|---|---|---|---|
| | ☐ | ☐ | ☐ | ☐ |

II. How many ASTD conferences have you attended?

| 0 | 1 | 2 | 3-5 | 10 or more |
|---|---|---|---|---|
| ☐ | ☐ | ☐ | ☐ | ☐ |

III. Professional Classification

| Corporate T&D | Government | Consultant | Vendor | Other |
|---|---|---|---|---|
| ☐ | ☐ | ☐ | ☐ | ☐ |

IV. Area of Concentration

| S&M | OD | Media | T&S | C&D | Int'l |
|---|---|---|---|---|---|
| ☐ | ☐ | ☐ | ☐ | ☐ | ☐ |

V. Session Evaluation

| | Yes | Somewhat | No |
|---|---|---|---|
| 1. Did this session match Program Book description | ☐ | ☐ | ☐ |
| 2. Will you apply this session directly in your work? | ☐ | ☐ | ☐ |
| 3. Did the speaker(s) use good communication skills? | ☐ | ☐ | ☐ |
| 4. Was there an appropriate level of audience participation for session objectives? | ☐ | ☐ | ☐ |
| 5. Would you like the(se) speaker(s) on next year's Program? | ☐ | ☐ | ☐ |
| 6. Would you like to see this topic on next year's Program? | ☐ | ☐ | ☐ |

IV. General Comments

1. If you could suggest one thing to improve this session it would be _____
_____
_____

2. What are the significant strengths of this session? _____
_____
_____

173

## FINAL COMMENT SHEET

Name of Program _____ Date _____

1. How would you rate the overall program as an educational experience?
   - ☐ Excellent      Comments:
   - ☐ Very Good
   - ☐ Good
   - ☐ Fair
   - ☐ Poor

2. To what extent will it help you do a better job for your organization?
   - ☐ To a large extent      Comments:
   - ☐ To some extent
   - ☐ Very little

3. What were the major benefits you received? (Check as many as you wish.)
   - ☐ Helped confirm some of my ideas.
   - ☐ Presented new ideas and approaches.
   - ☐ Acquainted me with problems and solutions from other companies.
   - ☐ Gave me a good chance to look objectively at myself and my job.
     Comments:

4. How were the meeting facilities?
   - ☐ Excellent      Comments:
   - ☐ Very Good
   - ☐ Good
   - ☐ Fair
   - ☐ Poor

### Using Critical Observers as Evaluators

The best way to get a professional evaluation is to have professional trainers evaluate the presenters. If you are making a presentation and there has been no arrangement for professional evaluation, make your own. Ask a peer to act as a critical observer and appraise your performance.

When you are responsible for the evaluation of a program, select a panel of three or four observers. Provide them with an instructor evaluation form and ask them to observe and evaluate the presenter. After the program, they can provide each instructor with a composite of their group evaluation.

The following is a suggested evaluation form for use by the observers. You may wish to alter it or develop your own evaluation form.

## INSTRUCTOR EVALUATION FORM

1. Statement of objectives
   a) ___not clear  ___barely clear  ___clear  ___very clear
   b) Tested student's reactions  ___yes  ___no
   c) Checked student's background  ___yes  ___no

2. Use of learning principles
   a) Participation techniques?  ___none  ___a few  ___just right
      ___too many
   b) Related to past experiences of group?  ___yes  ___no
   c) Interest-building techniques?  ___not used  ___a few used
      ___many used
   d) Provided opportunities for students to practice?  ___yes  ___no
   e) Presented a problem or challenge to the group?  ___yes  ___no
   f) Explained relationship between the various elements of the
      presentation?
      ___yes  ___no

3. Instructional techniques
   a) Check the techniques that were used.
      ___buzz group  ___demonstration  ___group activity
      ___role play  ___others
   b) Did the technique used clearly illustrate the instructor's point?
      ___yes  ___no

4. Use of visual aids
   a) List aid used _____
   b) Did the aid effectively add to the participant's understanding of the
      presentation?  ___yes  ___no

5. Design of lesson plan
   a) Organization?  ___poor  ___fair  ___good  ___very good
      ___excellent
   b) Transitions?  ___poor  ___fair  ___good  ___very good
      ___excellent
   c) Directed at specific objectives?  ___yes  ___no
   d) Interesting and informative?  ___no  ___barely  ___yes
      ___excellent
   e) Summary related material to objectives?  ___yes  ___no

6. Platform skills
    a) Voice?___poor ___fair ___good ___excellent
    b) Gestures? ___poor ___fair ___good ___excellent
    c) Style? ___poor ___fair ___good ___excellent

7. Management and control
    a) Management of time and materials? ___poor ___fair ___good ___excellent
    b) Control of group? ___poor ___fair ___good ___excellent

8. Suggested improvements: _____

_____

_____

## EVALUATING THE TRAINEE'S REACTION

There are three easily measured areas that will provide feedback on the impact of the program on the trainee. The three are: (1) trainee's reaction, in terms of feelings and opinions about the program, (2) the learning, and (3) the attitudinal change.

### Determining Trainee Reactions—The First Evaluation Area

The way the trainees feel about the training program is vitally important to the continuation of the program. As soon as they are back on the job, they will comment on and be questioned about the program. The feelings and opinions they express will be rapidly communicated throughout the organization. Favorable reports can ensure the continuation of the program. Whatever the participants' feelings are, positive or negative, you need to know so that you can use them to improve the program or to convince management of its value.

Written questionnaires are best for written reports. With these, you have the back-up evidence on file to support your evaluation. Questionnaires are ideally suited for collecting trainee feelings and opinions. Questionnaires can be designed with open-ended questions so that trainees are free to respond in their own words and express their own feelings.

The following are examples of open-ended questions that might be used to measure student reactions:

How do you feel about the opening session?

What do you think about . . . ?

What is your opinion . . . ?

How do you think we could improve . . . ?

How would you rate the various parts of the program?

### Testing Trainee Learning—The Second Evaluation Area

Pretesting and posttesting are reliable methods for determining what learning has occurred as a result of the program. A single test (posttest) at the end of a program may tell you what the students know but it doesn't tell you where they learned it. The trainees may have known it before they came to the program. To test what learning occurred in the program, administer the same type of test, similar in content, both at the beginning (pretest) and at the conclusion (posttest) of the program.

There are four basic techniques that may be used to test learning. They are the written test, the demonstration, problem discussion, and role play. The use of the written test is obvious. Demonstration by the student of the new skills gives the instructor a firsthand opportunity to evaluate the student's learning. By asking for student demonstrations, you are able to identify problem areas and help correct them before the program is concluded.

Program discussion is another way to test the participants' learning. By posing a problem for the students to solve in small group discussion sessions, you can observe and evaluate the knowledge and skills they apply to the problem. The problem should be designed so that its solution requires the knowledge, skills, and facts covered in the program.

### Testing Trainee Attitude Changes—The Third Evaluation Area

In role play, a student is asked to act out a part in a specific situation. Role play is similar to demonstration except that it usually requires interaction with another person. You might ask a student to play the role of a supervisor who has to explain some new techniques to the work group. The other participants play the part of the work group. You evaluate the change in attitude by having students engage in role play before and after instruction. By observing how the trainees treat each other in the before and after role plays, you can measure their attitudinal change.

### EVALUATING ON-THE-JOB RESULTS

The objective of training is to improve on-the-job results. In the final analysis, if your training programs are effective, they should result in such things as improved profits or the elimination of factors that would reduce profits. If you train current employees to be more productive, then profits eventually will increase. If you train new employees to meet standards quickly and minimize mistakes, or if you reduce the turnover rate, you help eliminate the factors that reduce profits. To evaluate training's impact on profits, you must evaluate behavioral change and productivity changes on the job.

Earlier, we used the questionnaire attitudes and perceptions, and the pretest and posttest to evaluate learning. Now we will use observation to evaluate behavioral change and a control group to evaluate effectiveness or productivity. These four tools may be laid out in chart form as a reminder.

| *Instrument* | *Evaluates* |
|---|---|
| • Pretest and posttest | • Learning |
| • Questionnaire | • Attitudes, opinions, and perceptions |
| • Observation | • Behavioral change and use of skills |
| • Control group | • Productivity and overall effectiveness |

### Evaluating Behavior Change

Behavioral change is measurable by observation on a before-and-after basis. Generally a trainee's peers, subordinates, or superiors will be most likely to notice and be able to report on changes in behavior. Unless they have been asked to rate specific characteristics before and after the training, however, their evaluation is likely to be vague and unreliable.

The following items, altered by the objectives of your program, might be used in before-and-after evaluations of a trainee's behavior.

- Application of new knowledge

- Use of new skills

- High standards

- Courtesy

- Adherence to safety regulations

- Teamwork

- Perseverance

- Honesty

- Cooperation

- Quality of work

- Punctuality

- Effort

- Initiative

An application of modern technology in evaluating behavioral change is the use of videotape recorders. The ideal prerecording would be to show the trainee's activities on the job with the video equipment. The trainee's behavior would be somewhat altered, however, if he or she knew the cameras were there.

The best way to use video recordings to check before-and-after behavior is to conduct role plays at the beginning and at the end of the program. Prepare role-play material that closely resembles the real work situation. Build in a problem or enough stress to require the trainee to devote full attention to the problem. Then the trainee will forget the audience and the video equipment, and will behave normally.

## Evaluating Productivity Changes

There are a number of factors that affect productivity or profits. An improvement in any one of them may result from training. You need only identify and relate your training objectives to them and then evaluate those specific factors after the training has been completed. If you can show management that training is responsible for improving profit, you will gain their support for future training programs.

The following are factors that should be considered in evaluating results or productivity changes.

- Direct cost reductions

- Grievance reductions

- Productivity of trained versus untrained employees

- Productivity after versus before training

- Work quality

- Quantitative results

- Accident rates

- Absenteeism

- Employee suggestions

- Supervisory ratings

- Profits

- Sales volumes

- Turnover rates
- Customer complaints
- Worker efficiency
- Training time required for proficiency
- Cost per untrained employee
- New product development
- New customers
- Public relations

## AN EIGHT-STEP SYSTEM FOR EVALUATING RESULTS

Training programs must provide skills that the trainee can use on the job. This means the trainee must accept the ideas presented as well as understand them. If a trainee practices a skill and doesn't remember the rationale for applying the skill, he or she may drift back into previously established patterns. When evaluating productivity six months or a year after a training program, it's a good idea to check understanding and acceptance at the same time. The following eight steps should include tests for understanding and acceptance.

1. *Trainees report their own results.* Give the trainees a report form at the workshop to fill out and return thirty days after they have completed the program. The trainees report the results and/or problems they encountered using the techniques learned at the workshop. If all the trainees are located in the same city, a follow-up meeting should be held. They bring their reports to the meeting and get feedback from other trainees on their results. Generally, the positive results far outweigh the problems.

2. *Prepare pretraining and posttraining productivity reports.* This comparison can be done for the month before and the month after the completion of training or for some other equal periods. We have used the four weeks before and the four weeks after consistently as this also gives us a history with which to compare current results. Use regular production reports if available; if not, you will have to arrange for special records to be kept for the comparative periods.

3. *Supervisory observation.* After sixty days back on the job, the trainees should have leveled off to a skill level that is comfortable for them. At this point, ask the supervisor to spend a day working with the person

to evaluate progress. In some jobs it may be necessary to spend a longer time with the trainee to fully evaluate performance.

The supervisor should keep records and reports on the trainee's results as well as the understanding of concepts, attitudes, and skills. The report should compare the trainee's skills to those of other workers and should point out the trainee's strengths and weaknesses. The supervisor should also recommend areas that require further training. Retraining may be provided for major weaknesses at this point.

4. *Usefulness and self-evaluation questionnaire.* After ninety days back on the job, the trainee should be asked to evaluate the usefulness of the training and how well she or he is doing. The questions should be designed to elicit the trainee's attitudes as well as the understanding and use of the skills. The following are simple questions that might be used:

a) Describe what you believe to be *the best way* to complete job X.

b) Describe the way *you actually* do complete job X.

c) Have your skills improved or deteriorated as a result of the training program?

d) What results have you achieved that are related directly to the new skills that you learned in training?

e) Elaborate on any problems or successes you have had as a result of your training.

5. *Manager's productivity report.* At the end of six months, after training, the trainee's manager should be asked for a productivity report. This report not only helps you evaluate the results of training, but also brings the results to the attention of management, which helps sell training. This report is directed at productivity changes. Ask for a six-month comparison of profits, costs, and other improvements that the training program covered.

6. *Filing of unsolicited reports.* If your program is a good one, you will receive many unsolicited reports. There will be letters or notes commending the program. File these reports and refer to them when making your own written evaluation of the program. You will also get verbal comments praising your program and requests for future training. Make a note with the date and file these requests for later use. You may need the names of those who requested a specific program to get approval for it later.

7. *Using a new program to evaluate the previous one.* If you conduct a pretest at the beginning of a new program, you can use it to evaluate retained learning. Write questions into the pretest that cover the atti-

tudes, skills, and understanding of concepts covered in the previous seminar. The answers to these questions can be compared to those given at the end of the previous seminar. This system can be used continually, over time, depending on how often you have people back for additional training sessions.

8. *Conduct role plays in the new program that require the use of skills learned in the previous program.* Again, design the role play to test the attitudes, understanding, and skills covered in the previous program. As the participants act out the role, they will reveal their attitudes and you will be able to observe their skills and determine their understanding by carefully monitoring the role plays.

These eight steps may not be the perfect system for you. Every training program has unique qualities and unique objectives. You should be able to adapt our ideas to your objectives and develop your own system. The perfect system for you is the one that measures results in relation to your objectives.

## SUMMARY

There are four generally accepted parts of evaluation. These are reaction, learning, behavior, and results. To be effective and useful, evaluation must cover every element in the program, beginning with program design and continuing through on-the-job performance results. This can best be accomplished by evaluating individually the following key elements:

- Program
- Presenter
- Participants
- Performance

# The All-Star Trainer

*Always shoot for the moon, because even if you miss, you'll still end up among the stars.*

That piece of advice holds very true not only in training but in life as well. By striving for perfection or self-achievement, we can make all of our efforts "star" activities.

And yet we see so many training sessions and other general business activities that simply fall short of their mark. The sad part of most of these failures is that with just a little more effort, a bit more preparation, or a few more minutes of planning, the activity could have been an excellent one.

When you really think about an extraordinarily well done effort, all it is really is an ordinary task with just a bit of "extra" effort. This is what the "All-Star Trainer" is all about.

We've all been involved in attending training sessions, service club meetings, small group meetings, and other types of gatherings in which we listen to a speaker. Some sessions go well; some go very poorly. What makes the difference?

In a word, it's the trainer.

This chapter will build the foundation of the All-Star Trainer by offering a visual aid for those of you who might also be involved in training other trainers. We will explore some basic elements for the All-Star and also discuss those traits exhibited by a "falling star." By looking at those personal qualities of an effective instructor, you will learn which items are most looked for as described by participants in actual training situations.

## THE STAR

What separates the star from one who is mediocre? What makes one instructor's classes always "fill" while a colleague talks to a half-empty room? In brief, what goes into building a star trainer?

The key words are the three Bs—Base, Blend, and Brighten.

*Base.* Base your level of instruction at the level of the group. If you recall the definition of *communication* in Chapter 8, we said that communication was for "expression," *not* for "impression." Too many times these terms are confused. We can't communicate very effectively by talking down to trainees—or, for that matter, to anyone! Every once in a while, we'll observe a trainer who is so determined to impress (rather than express) that the big 50-cent and 75-cent words are used far too often. While these types of words may sound eloquent and sophisticated, they should not be used if they are not understood. For example, this statement taken verbatim from an educator's report: "Perhaps the task of developing proper motivation extrinsic factors to that of keeping homeostatic needs and exterioceptive drive low, in favor of facilitating basic information processing to maximize accurate anticipation of reality" really means if you want to keep them interested, teach them something!

Be careful, too, to watch the jargon and technical language, which is so much a part of every organization. While "Form 2517" or "MBO" or "SOR-16" may be common terms to you, don't assume your participants have that same understanding.

Your session content should be relevant, of course, and adapted to the backgrounds and experiences of your participants.

*Blend.* Blend your instructional content with the backgrounds and experiences of your participants. As your group continues to build from their own experiences, new subject matter, skills, or attitudes, your blending of these items helps make their learning that much more effective. As they grasp new material and recognize how it can be neatly added to their existing body of information, they are practicing the principle of self-learning. As they begin to realize that regardless of age or experience, they *can* learn, your participants may enthusiastically become more vocally active in the session and help you ensure the practicality and relevance of your content.

*Brighten.* Brighten your session by using a variety of instructional aids and methods. Vary your methods by using lecture, discussion, cases, and role play as your lesson plan suggests. Coupled with visuals, an otherwise boring session can come alive. With the use of different methods of instruction, participants will more likely keep pace with you. A refreshing change of pace not only seems to make the time pass faster, but your group is more likely to stay interested. An enthusiastic trainer can instill a like enthusiasm in the group. With such an atmosphere in the training session, learning is easier and more interesting. As we have said, people learn best in a warm and friendly atmosphere. A variety of techniques and an enthusiastic presentation will build a climate conducive to a good learning experience.

## Traits

In a continuing attempt to identify the traits and characteristics of the "All-Star Trainer," dozens of groups were asked to do just that. Participants attending "Train-the-Trainer" workshops across the country conducted by the authors listed the qualities they felt were most important. In addition to enumerating these sought-after traits, the participants were further asked to identify the *one* most important skill characteristic of the Star Trainer.

As might be expected, there is no consensus of opinion. However, two traits always seem to come out on top. These two top traits are: 1) Ability to communicate and 2) Knowledge of subject matter.

Since we've already covered the importance of communication in an earlier chapter, we need not do so here.

Let's discuss the other qualities listed by the workshop participants:

*Knowledge of subject.* Participants have every right to expect their instructors to know their subjects thoroughly. This means the instructors are well prepared when they enter the training room. Subject matter must be well planned and completely understood by the trainer before it can ever be effectively communicated to the audience.

While it is acknowledged that thorough knowledge is almost imperative, no one person could be expected to know *everything* on any given topic. In those cases when a question may be posed by a trainee and the instructor simply does not know the answer, it is important to note the suggested manner of response. In most situations, the best answer is an honest and forthright "I don't know." This candid response is then followed by a promise to check out the answer and report it back at the next session or earliest possible time.

Another response may be to throw the question right back at the group. Often, the background or experience of the group itself may offer a good response to the discussion at hand. Moreover, a comment or idea expressed by a group member may trigger an idea for the trainer also.

*Adaptability.* Top trainers exhibit the quality of being able to adapt their training to the needs of the trainees. This flexibility refers to the quick and ready changes that may have to be made in the lesson plan, the presentation, or anything else that occurs with the training program. These are often on-the-spot decisions that must be made. This is not to imply that one or two isolated comments by a trainee should persuade the instructor to depart completely from the scheduled objectives. It does, however, dictate that if the instructor determines that the session content is clearly not geared to the needs, interests, or backgrounds of the majority of the members of this particular group, then a change in approach or content is very definitely required.

In sales training, this statement is used: "To sell John Smith on what he buys, sell John Smith through John Smith's eyes."

In other words, everything that happens in the training facility must be done from—and for—the interest of the trainee. The most important word in the English language is "you." Therefore, it would follow that the trainer must gear the presentation to the needs of the participants.

*Sincerity.* Trainees appreciate the real and honest show of sincerity in their instructors. By exhibiting a deep and serious interest in the field of human resource development and being completely professional in the performance of all the varied tasks in the training situation, the star trainer will appear totally dedicated and sincere.

*Sense of humor.* Learning can be fun. In discussions with trainees enumerating most-desired qualities in their trainers, a sense of humor is invariably mentioned. This is not to say we are looking for an entertainer or a clown, but rather someone who really enjoys the work. Very often, a point can be made with a story or anecdote. Humorous stories should be told primarily if they can be related to a point being discussed.

Many trainers begin a new training session with a story or two to "warm up" the group in an attempt to create an atmosphere of informality. Off-color jokes or sexist stories are *never* acceptable. Further, if you are not comfortable telling stories, you are well advised to not even try. It's always your own best judgment that should prevail.

*Interest.* The Star Trainer is interested and interesting. This interest is keen and readily felt by the group. The nonverbal communication cues that we may not even realize we're sending are observed and read by the group. If the presenter is careless or slovenly with handouts, discussion items, or literally anything in or about the training session, these signs come through loud and clear. The group might feel, "If the instructor doesn't care—why should I?"

*Understanding and willingness to involve group.* We have already made the point that effective learning must involve the student. This means that the two-way communication discussed in Chapter 9 is always part of your instructional technique.

If your group is one that you, as the trainer, don't really know prior to the sessions, it is well worth your time to make every effort to get to know your people. Some instructors use a simple questionnaire or survey form filled out prior to, or at, the first session. With such information, they can obtain some background on their participants.

You may prefer to gather this information from the participants at the first session. Perhaps during the introductions of the participants, you will ask them to offer this information as they introduce themselves. You might consider using a written form even with verbal introductions, since many participants may be reluctant to tell too much of their background or experience for fear of "showing off" in front of their peers.

But merely knowing this background information is of little value. As you review the trainees' experiences, determine how their backgrounds and areas of expertise can benefit other participants as well as yourself. During discussion on relevant items, ask the respective individuals how their real world experience fortifies or strengthens a point. Lively discussion and learning can also result when one's background may differ from or seem to negate your points. This is to be expected, and you shouldn't let a contrary point upset you. Quickly throw both points of view back to the group for further discussion. If ensuing discussion further disputes your own experience or lesson plan, recognize the opposing viewpoints and continue on with the presentation. If you are, in fact, operating on a wrong assumption or incorrect premise, admit it freely, but don't apologize or get carried away with excuses. Your participants will respect your acknowledgment of error and more than likely will strongly empathize with you.

Getting back to our main point of group involvement, remember that learning is not a spectator sport. The more active participation in guided discussions, the better the learning experience.

*Clear instruction.* A person conceivably might know just about all there is to know about a given subject, but if that person does not possess good communication skills, that wealth of knowledge cannot be transmitted to others. Talking *with*—not *at*—the group is a communication skill. Review the four-step method of teaching:

1. Prepare

2. Present

3. Participate

4. Summarize

Prepare your session by preparing yourself and the group. Present the information in easy-to-digest pieces. Use participation and group involvement to enhance the learning effort. Finally, summarize and review what has been covered to help your participants learn more easily.

To further amplify the importance of clear and articulate instruction, remember the item mentioned in Chapter 9 regarding the efficiency of communications. Studies indicated that as much as 70 percent of our communication efforts can be misunderstood, mistaken, missed, or messed! An astute trainer makes certain the group understands and accepts the two-pronged elements of communication.

*Individual assistance.* The Star Trainer is willing to assist the individual participant in—and out—of the classroom. In large groups, a person who finds the instruction at too advanced a level may be hesitant to say so in the training session. By being observant and by actively exhibiting the desire to give individualized attention, the trainer communicates a feeling of interest for each individual in the session. Even though an individual may not vocally state a problem in staying up with the instructional pace, the Star Trainer is alert to the nonverbal cues of that person, and also listens to participants during breaks, between sessions, and so on. By making your time available for questions, additional help, or other individual assistance, you are showing your group that you *are* interested in them. You are also showing your colleagues and superiors that "training" is more than just a job, and you are already well on your way to becoming professional in your activities.

*Practicality of subject matter.* Another trait mentioned by participants in training sessions deals with the practicality of the subject matter. The best trainer always attempts to make the session as pragmatic and as "down-to-earth" as possible. While it may be necessary to discuss theory or academic material for background or foundation purposes, most participants are problem oriented, not fact oriented. Constantly show how the information you present is related to their job responsibilities. Practicality is the byword.

*Enthusiasm.* Nothing is more pleasantly contagious than the quality of enthusiasm in a trainer. A dynamic presentation and a vibrant personality show your participants that your profession—people helping people—is the most important activity in the universe. This is easier said than done, particularly if yours is a session repeated over and over again.

Participants tend to respond in kind to an enthusiastic climate. The entire atmosphere of the training session becomes alive and your group is more inclined to want to learn.

*Other personal qualities.* There are several other qualities that participants look for in their trainers. They want a person who can facilitate group learning without appearing to overly direct the exercise. Personal traits of promptness, neatness, friendliness, and courtesy are all important. The ability to create a desire and interest in the learning process is an excellent quality. And certainly, a modulated voice with good English and proper grammar is essential.

## THE FALLING STAR

While most of your efforts will be "star" presentations and some may be "superstar," hopefully none will be a "falling star." To make sure we will avoid the falling-star syndrome, here are the items participants have indicated they dislike seeing in their instructors. As you would guess, most of these are the corollary to our All-Star list.

*Superiority.* Trainees rightfully resent an air of snobbery or superiority. They fully realize that their knowledge of the subject matter is less than the instructor's, but they intensely dislike being talked down to! Trainers—and trainees—can learn from each other with the proper learning climate. Differences of age, background, and experience can be dispensed with if trainers and trainees understand that learning is truly a collaborative process. For one person, namely the trainer, to relegate the trainee to a subordinate level is to disregard a basic concept of mutual respect.

*Lack of knowledge.* As earlier intimated, the exploding rate of total knowledge makes it literally impossible for any one single individual to know everything about everything! Your participants expect you to have a high degree of knowledge in your chosen field of specialization, but there may be an occasional time when you may be stumped by a question. Don't get flustered if a question is posed to which you honestly don't have a response. Ask the group if any of them have had any experience along the lines of the unanswered question. If no response, admit your lack of knowledge freely, suggest you will attempt to find a suitable answer, and go on with your presentation.

Obviously if these incidents occur frequently, you'll want to spend additional time in preparation and gain more knowledge.

*Unclear teaching.* Participants are quick to point out they are not fond of trainers who do not teach clearly. Inarticulate presentations, poor speech habits, and other unsatisfactory communication traits detract from learning.

*Indifference.* An indifferent attitude toward self, participants, or your work can be quickly observed by your group. A trainee tends to think, "If the trainer doesn't care about this class, how can he (or she) possibly care about me?" This air of insolence and indifference is a serious one. It carries over into all facets of the training program and may even permeate the entire human resource department. Rightly or wrongly, participants make those judgments. Indifference is communicated nonverbally and these cues are unmistakenly read by the group.

*Impatience.* People do learn at different speeds and it is imperative that the trainer remember this. Put yourself in the place of a new trainee who is a bit slow to grasp the ideas or content of the session. How would you like to be on the receiving end of an impatient, growling trainer insinuating that you are a slow learner? There may be a reason for the lack of comprehension—physical or psychological, mental or manual. Be patient and always watch your temper.

*Physical qualities.* A monotonous voice, a listless attitude, and a slovenly appearance are but a few of the physical traits that turn participants away from a learning atmosphere. There have been too many times when an otherwise excellent session has been lessened by an indifferent trainer. A well-designed and carefully drawn out lesson plan is virtually worthless if it is carried to the participants by a trainer who is merely "going through the motions." Remember, too, that first impressions are lasting ones; and your physical appearance communicates to your new participants—in a matter of seconds—what kind of person you are and what kind of program you're instructing. Rightly or wrongly, people do make these snap judgments.

## SEVEN STEPS TO STARDOM

Here you are, ready to embark on an exciting and challenging assignment. You are now about to join the ranks of a special group of people—human resource development professionals.

In these final few pages of this book, we'd like to offer you, by way of review, several proven points that you can use as tips to better training. These have been covered in many ways throughout these pages in different chapters. It is helpful, however, to itemize them as a final summary for your consideration. These are not theoretical principles based on academic research; they are tested points proven through hundreds of training programs conducted by your authors. As you gain experience in this dynamic field, you will find your success may well depend on how you use and practice these seven steps to stardom.

1. *Trainees must want to learn.* As you learned in Chapter 10 on motivation, there is only one way to get anyone to do anything—and that is to make that person *want* to do it. Simple as this must certainly sound, there is no other way! The learning climate must be conducive to good learning. Learning, as you know, is largely a self-activity. By providing the proper motivational climate, you enable your participants to establish their own desires and motivation. By letting them know why a task or job is important, you are essentially telling your people *they* are important too!

   By learning new techniques, your participants may find their jobs are made easier. "Work smarter, not harder" is the keystone for work simplification.

2. *We learn best by doing.* The more we involve the use of the senses, the more we can learn. The "hands-on" or "show and tell" exercises in which our participants gain firsthand experience are best for retention. As involvement increases, learning increases. On-the-job training is effective because of the real world activity being learned through actual

performance. To verify the importance of involvement, consider this fact of retention:

We will remember 5 to 10 percent of what we see; 30 to 50 percent of what we see and hear; 50 to 70 percent of what we say; 70 to 90 percent of what we do and say.

As these figures indicate, we must involve our participants as much as possible, visually and mentally, to let them learn more effectively.

3. *Adults will learn what they need to learn.* Although you can force-feed your training, you cannot force learning. If a participant does not recognize the desire or acknowledge the need to learn, it is all but impossible to force that individual to learn. Properly motivated, trainees can learn if they feel a need to learn. Give them the skills, attitudes, and knowledge they need and can put to use right now! Practicality is the key word and immediacy of application is often paramount. While some sessions may rightfully teach the "nice to know," participants will respond better to the things they "need to know."

4. *Use problem-centered learning.* Your participants will learn faster and better if you use actual business or organizational problems and let them work out the solutions. Often, you can derive some basic principles "after the fact." This type of inductive reasoning is extremely well suited to mature groups. The discovery of knowledge or the formulation of principles through the case-study method is an excellent approach. Role playing also uses the same basis for learning. The inductive process may start with a specific problem that is discussed by the group. After thorough analysis and discussion guided by the leader, certain principles may be deduced. Realistic problems or cases are good learning vehicles since their relevance and practicality are obvious. The rote learning of facts and figures has little place in most adult learning situations.

5. *Experience connotes learning.* Since we know adults learn from each other, it behooves us to capitalize on the backgrounds and experience of our group. Exploit this wealth of talent and expertise in a positive way. Make use of the experience through discussion and group participation. If new knowledge coincides with their past experiences, that reinforcement makes a more forceful impact. If your comments are fortified and validated by concrete examples offered by group members, the other participants will react and learn more easily. No one likes a "know-it-all," and don't mistake your own role as one that has all the answers. When questions are asked of you, turn the questions back to the group first and let the experience of a participant help frame an

answer. By skillfully building a series of questions and answers you can help guide the group to your stated objective.

6. *Keep things informal.* It is a proven fact that adults will learn best in an atmosphere of informality. The physical arrangements of your training facility will do much to help or hinder the training effort. Vary the seating arrangement and use the theater style only on rare occasions. Provide for smoking and no smoking sections if possible. Keep things informal, yet businesslike. Your own behavior and dress will set the stage for the entire group. Learning seldom takes place in a hostile environment; learning often occurs in a warm, congenial atmosphere. Let informality be your key word.

7. *Give them variety.* Artful use of visuals, coupled with a fast-paced presentation, makes for a good learning climate. A variety of methods and techniques helps ensure a learning experience. Group participation is a very effective tool for learning; the lecture is perhaps least effective. However, each has its place dependent on time and goals. Spice up your presentation with different visual aids. By so doing, you are providing the ingredients for a better training session.

## SUMMARY

We've all seen living examples of the All-Star Trainer. Sad to state, we've probably seen some versions of the negative counterpart as well. By knowing what qualities participants look for in trainers, you can emulate these traits to make your presentation better. It's important, too, to alert ourselves to those negative items that "turn off" participants. Since trainees will seldom verbalize these "falling-star" items, the listing is needed.

Finally, the "seven steps to stardom" are nothing more than a recap and review of this entire volume. Keep these tips in mind always and your every session will truly be All Star!

# SELECTED REFERENCES

Albrecht, Karl. *Brainpower*. Englewood Cliffs, N.J.: Prentice-Hall, Inc., 1980.

Anderson, Ronald H. *Selecting and Developing Media for Instruction*. 2d ed. New York: Van Nostrand Reinhold, 1982.

Bennis, Warren, and Burt Nanus. *Leaders: The Strategies for Taking Charge*. New York: Harper & Row, 1985.

Blake, Robert R., and Jane Mouton. *Synergogy*. San Francisco, California: Jossey-Bass, 1984.

Blank, W.E. *Handbook for Developing Competency-Based Training Programs*. Englewood Cliffs, N.J.: Prentice-Hall, Inc., 1982.

Carnevale, Anthony P., and Harold Goldstein. *Employee Training: Its Changing Role and an Analysis of New Data*. Washington, D.C.: ASTD Press, 1983.

Chalofsky, Neal, and Carnie Ives Lincoln. *Up the HRD Ladder*. Reading, Mass.: Addison-Wesley, 1983.

Craig, Robert L. ed. *The Training and Development Handbook*. 2d ed. New York: McGraw-Hill Book Company, 1976.

Davis, Ivor K. *Instructional Technique*. New York: McGraw-Hill Book Company, 1981.

Deming, Basil S. *Evaluating Job-Related Training*. Englewood Cliffs, N.J.: Prentice-Hall, Inc., 1982.

Desatnick, Robert L. *The Business of Human Resource Management*. New York: John Wiley & Sons, 1982.

Donaldson, Les. *Behavioral Supervision*. Reading, Mass.: Addison-Wesley, 1980.

Dyer, William G. *Contemporary Issues in Management and Organization Development*. Reading, Mass.: Addison-Wesley, 1982.

Fombrun, Charles, Noel M. Tichy, and Mary Anne Devanna. *Strategic Human Resource Management*. New York: John Wiley & Sons, 1985.

Gael, Sidney. *Job Analysis: A Guide to Assessing Work Activities*. San Francisco, California: Jossey-Bass, 1983.

Houle, Cyril O. *Patterns of Learning*. San Francisco, California: Jossey-Bass, 1984.

Jeffries, James R., and Jefferson D. Bates. *The Executive's Guide to Meetings, Conferences & Audio-Visual Presentation*. New York: McGraw-Hill Book Company, 1983.

Kearsley, Greg. *Computer-Based Training: A Handbook for Human Resource Development*. Reading, Mass.: Addison-Wesley, 1983.

————. *Costs, Benefits and Productivity in Training Systems*. Reading, Mass.: Addison-Wesley, 1982.

————. *Training and Technology: A Handbook for HRD Professionals*. Reading, Mass.: Addison-Wesley, 1984.

Kirkpatrick, Donald L. *Evaluating Training Programs*. Washington, D.C.: ASTD Press, 1973.

———. *How to Improve Performance Through Appraisal and Coaching*. New York: AMACOM, 1982.

———. *A Practical Guide for Supervisory Training and Development*. 2d ed. Reading, Mass.: Addison-Wesley, 1984.

Knowles, M.S. *The Adult Learner: A Neglected Species*. Houston: Gulf Publishing Co., 1978.

———. *Andragogy in Action*. San Francisco, California: Jossey-Bass, 1984.

Laird, Dugan D., and R. House. *Interactive Classroom Instruction*. Glenview, Ill.: Scott Foresman & Co., 1984.

Lambert, Clark. *The Complete Book of Supervisory Training*. New York: John Wiley & Sons, 1984.

———. *Secrets of a Successful Trainer: A Simplified Guide for Survival in the Classroom*. New York: John Wiley & Sons, 1986.

Mager, R.F. *Preparing Instructional Objectives*. Revised 2d ed. Belmont, California: Pitman Learning, 1984.

———. *Troubleshooting the Troubleshooting Course*. Belmont, California: Pitman Learning, Inc., 1982.

McLagan, Patricia A. *Helping Others Learn: Designing Programs for Adults*. Reading, Mass.: Addison-Wesley, 1982.

———. *Models for Excellence: The Conclusions and Recommendations of the ASTD Training and Development Competency Study*. Washington, D.C.: ASTD Press, 1983.

Munson, Lawrence. *How to Conduct Training Seminars for Management, Marketing, Sales, Technical and Educational Seminars*. New York: McGraw-Hill Book Company, 1984.

Nadler, Leonard. *Designing Training Programs. The Critical Events Model*. Reading, Mass.: Addison-Wesley, 1982.

———, ed. *The Handbook of Human Resource Development*. New York: John Wiley & Sons, 1984.

Newstrom, John W., and Edward E. Scannell. *Games Trainers Play*. New York: McGraw-Hill Book Company, 1980.

Odiorne, George. *The Strategic Managing of Human Resources*. San Francisco, California: Jossey-Bass, 1984.

Peters, Thomas J., and Robert H. Waterman, Jr. *In Search of Excellence*. New York: Harper & Row, 1982.

Scannell, Edward E. *Supervisory Communications*. Dubuque, Iowa: Kendall-Hunt Publishing Co., 1982.

———, and John W. Newstrom. *More Games Trainers Play*. New York: McGraw-Hill Book Company, 1984.

Smith, Barry J., and Brian L. Delahaye. *How to Be an Effective Trainer: Skills for Managers and New Trainers*. New York: John Wiley & Sons, 1984.

Taylor, Barnard, and Gordon Lippitt. *Management Development and Training Handbook*. 2d ed. New York: McGraw-Hill Book Company, 1982.

Tracey, William R. ed. *Human Resources Management and Development Handbook*. New York: AMACOM, 1983.

## Selected References

Wlodkowski, Raymond J. *Enhancing Adult Motivation to Learn*. San Francisco, California: Jossey-Bass, 1985.

Zemke, Ron. *Figuring Things Out*. Reading, Mass.: Addison-Wesley, 1982.

Additional books, articles, audio and videotapes in the field of human resource development are available from:
ASTD Press
American Society for Training and Development
1630 Duke Street
Box 1443
Alexandria, VA 22313